IT'S NOT ABOUT YOU

A Scriptural Invitation to Community

For Aunt Bev,
Thanks for all the support
through the years!, Ryan

RYAN FORTNER

First published by Ryan Fortner in 2018

ISBN-13: 978-1974560646
ISBN-10: 1974560643

Book cover design: Clayton Cover (www.claytoncover.com)
clayton.cover@gmail.com

Contents

About The Authors

Ryan Fortner is a recent graduate of Mount Vernon Nazarene University where he earned a B.A. in Intercultural Studies and minored in Political Science. *It's Not About Us* is his first publication. He is currently serving in Lexington, Ohio as a youth pastor.

Hank Spaulding is a Doctoral Candidate at Garrett-Evangelical Theological Seminary. He is also an adjunct professor of Church History and Christian Ethics at Mount Vernon Nazarene University. He has published various articles and chapters in books including "The Lacerated God: Toward a Theology of Self Mutilation." He is also completing a book on the Sacraments entitled *Living the Body: Sacraments and Christian Material Existence*. He lives in Mount Vernon, Ohio.

Foreword: Prolegomena to Reading Scripture
By Hank Spaulding

How should we read the Bible? This is a fundamental question of the Christian faith. This already assumes that Christians *should* read the Bible but asks the manner in which one reads it. The context of this question is the historical struggle of Christianity to find an appropriate way to read its authoritative text. This means reading the Bible is a dangerous task. At once, reading the Bible can lead to the liberation of an oppressed people as in the Civil Rights Movement, or can lead to the enslavement of a people as in the context of Antebellum Slavery. To this end, I propose that the Bible should be read as Scripture. Though this seems like a heuristic statement, I argue that the distinction is crucial.

Theologian John Webster gives the clearest accounts of the Bible as Scripture. Scripture, as distinct from Bible, is a text that reveals the saving activity of God. As Webster writes, "both the texts and the processes surrounding their reception are subservient to the selfpresentation of the triune God...by which readers are accosted."[1] Scripture, thus, is a thing reality used for divine purposes.[2] However, reading the Bible as Scripture is not just a way of talking about the text, but also what it does. The Scripture also witnesses to a "saving fellowship"with God, namely God saves us to be with God.[3] Therefore, to read the Scriptures outside of this saving fellowship means to lose the significance of the text's purpose.[4]

Webster's analysis of Scripture's content could be summarized as: God saves. This is a simple summary of the entire narrative of Scripture. By qualifying Scripture within the salvation of God, Scripture enables a new community. Salvation is not merely a spiritual exchange but the establishing of a new communion between God and humankind. The possibilities of such a community are *revealed* in Scripture. To be clear, the agent of revelation is not Scripture, but God. However, the Scriptures witness to this salvation and the positing of new community distinctly from other creaturely realities.

The question begged at this juncture is this: Exactly where does Scripture fit in this formation of new creaturely possibilities? Scripture is a created gift from God, as a witness to God's self-presentation. In this approach to Scripture, the purpose is a submission to the text's unique ability to attest to this self-presentation of God. Therefore, this approach forms

---

1 John Webster, *Holy Scripture: A Dogmatic Sketch.* (New York: Cambridge University Press. 2003), 6.

2 Ibid, 8-9.

3 Ibid, 13.

4 Ibid, 68-106.

certain kinds of readers *of* the Scripture. Reading Scripture is essential for the community to surrender its own priority. To read Scripture means to become certain kind of readers.[5] Therefore, the Church consists of readers who are submitting to this text, and thus are confronted with divine speech and must be bound to others in community.

Reading Scripture as a document with unique ability to attest to the revelation of the triune God subordinates all other creaturely concerns to this task. So, for example, the work of reading Scripture is not to unleash oneself, but rather to submit oneself to Scripture. In so doing, this revelation overcomes human estrangement from God and one another. [6] Therefore, the church is not grounded in the human or in the individual, but in divine speech, namely the voice of the self-presentation of God.[7] God, through divine speech, as Webster sights above, continually accosts humanity and reorients them away from the dangers of themselves and toward a reality that they cannot control: God. This is a turn to God who confronts us on every page of the Scripture. Webster proposes that when one reads the Bible as Scripture one is "slain and made alive."[8] As Webster states,

> "*The rectitude of the will, its conformity to the matter of the gospel, is crucial, so that reading can only occur as a kind of brokenness, a*

---

5 Ibid, 88.

6 Ibid, 87-88.

7 Ibid, 83.

8 Ibid, 88.

relinquishment of willed mastery of the text, and through exegetical reading's guidance towards that encounter with God of which the text is an instrument." [9]

Therefore, reading Bible as Scripture is anti-selfish in its stand against the ways that the humans attempt to give the text meaning. Instead, reading Scripture looks to the text for the saving, self-presentation of God.

If we commit to Webster's account of Scripture located within God's life, then the path forward for humanity becomes closed. Rather, humanity must place itself under the internal logic of this narrative and thus be bound into the community it creates.

Therefore, the purpose of Ryan's study is toward this end. The God revealed in the beautifully mundane and consistently spectacular stories of the text should be read with an eye toward God, but also toward the community that God creates. This means that the divinely revealed text is for the purpose of informing our common life. To misread the text is precisely a refusal to be formed, namely a refusal to worship God.

---

9 Ibid.

Dear Reader

I wrote this book out of a personal realization that it is extremely easy to look past that which is right in front of us. What I mean is that too often I find myself trying to impose Scripture into my life rather than looking at what it might have meant when it was written. I have caught myself reading the Bible in order to enlighten my own life, but not to bring light to the One who it is all about. *It's Not About You* is focused inwardly as much as it is outwardly. In the following pages, I seek to engage with some overlooked aspects of Scriptural study by turning the focus away from the reader and back towards the Author. This is an appeal to the human spirit that wants to call out to that still, small voice inside each of us and say, "Here is an answer". It may not be The Answer, but it is something that has given me a great sense of peace in my own life and is something that I wish to share with every person that reads this book.

This is a presentation of an invitation. In the following pages, we will journey together through a conversation of how to study the Bible. Far too often, I have found myself coming to the Bible with a specific motive. Perhaps I need a question answered or my anxieties to be quieted and so I come to Scripture with a preconceived notion of what I am going to find. For a long time, I was completely content with my Biblical study mode of operation. That was until I realized that this way of doing things was all wrong. Someone once told me that if I say "well, Jesus used to hang out with sinners" as an excuse to go wherever I wanted and be with whoever I desired, then I was putting myself in the wrong place in that story. I am certainly not insinuating that Jesus would not want us to hang out with people who need Him, but this encounter did make me realize that I had been putting myself in Jesus' place in far too many instances. I am the sinner to whom Jesus is calling, not the Savior. It was then that I began to realize that in all my years of living what I perceived to be a good Christian life, I had been missing the most important point of all: Christianity is about Christ. None of it has ever been nor will ever be about me.

For the sake of simplicity and camaraderie, I feel that I should explain myself on a few stylistic choices I have made for this work. You'll notice that I choose to qualify God as 'He' throughout the book. I understand that some readers may not like the idea of assigning a gender to God, who is to be above all human distinction. My choice to qualify God as 'He' is not a comment on any theological standing, but a choice made to keep with the theme of God as Father. The choice to capitalize the first letter of the word used to signify God is simply to distinguish and show a form of respect to God when I am referring to Him. To be blunt, I just don't see the use in debating the theological significance of these choices, but I feel it would be best to point them out and explain my reasoning rather than let any sort of negativity build in you, the reader. There is far more to be concerned about than God's gender. I hope we understand each other.

And so, I present to you this book. It's a work born out of a life of misplaced intentions that is seeking to be righted again. In these chapters, I hope to pique your interest enough to compel you to continue your own journey with a few new thoughts. This is not the end of the process, but I hope it serves as a nudge in the right direction. I've written my heart into these pages, and I hope that at least one point that I've made will help you in some way to get to know Christ. Without further ado, *It's Not About You.*

Introduction

Deep within each of us there is a desire to be part of something bigger than ourselves and to make a lasting impact on humanity. I have yet to meet someone for whom this isn't true. This desire may not be intentional or even noticeable, but it stems from our primal impulse to do whatever it takes to live. As we come to terms with our mortality, we turn our striving towards the quest for a way to make our lives, or at least our memory, carry on long after we are gone. We want to feel that we have made a difference in the world, and that our lives have left an imprint on the stories of those around us. It is to that craving for some greater purpose that I respond with great news: God wants our lives to have a lasting impact too. Our Creator designed us to have an enduring influence on the world He created. The only tricky part is that our impact might not come exactly how we have always pictured. In the following pages, we are going to examine exactly what God desires for each of our lives by engaging with the Bible.

Oftentimes, we refer to the Bible as a guidebook for our lives. Any traveler knows that a guidebook is an invaluable resource to its followers. If we hold it in such high esteem, then we should take a serious look at what the Scriptures are guiding us toward, and how that could address our desire to make a difference. This book seeks to present a way of interpreting Scripture that depicts the Kingdom of God as the 'something bigger' for which we are all searching. To do so, we will examine the Bible through the lens of its original context to figure out what it might have meant to its original readers, we will consider what the existence of an eternal Kingdom means to us as participants, and we will look closely at a foundational belief of Christianity to see how the Trinity works to foster a genuine Community in a divided world.

The Bible is littered with statements regarding the Kingdom of God and declares the Creator as the ruler over this Kingdom. So, we need to figure out what exactly this Kingdom could be like before we can continue with any conversation about how to be part of it.

WHAT IS THE KINGDOM OF GOD?

It is a daunting task to try to describe the Kingdom of God in its entirety. What we can say for certain is that the Kingdom of God is the description of the rule of God over the entire universe. What we are discussing when we consider the Kingdom of God is the idea of a group of people over whom God has authority. While it is a physical kingdom, that is not the primary idea behind the Kingdom. Rather we should be focusing on the concept of a group of people, perhaps it is more correct to say all people, whom God has claimed as His own.

It would be natural to think that God's authority comes from having created us, but that is not the entire picture. While His authority is certain, when we talk about the Kingdom of God we need to realize that to really be part of the Kingdom we have to accept and submit to His authority. The Kingdom that Jesus describes in the Gospels is something different from all of Creation. God is not an overlord, and He does not rule with an iron fist. He is the Father of His children, and while He desires for every single one of us to enjoy His Kingdom, what we see in the Bible is a God that does not force anyone to accept the invitation. He does not force us to accept His rule over our lives. That is a choice that we must make for ourselves.

God will do, and has done, everything He can to extend the invitation to join Him in the Kingdom, and we see that invitation in Scripture. The Father desires for each person to be part of His Kingdom because, simply put, He loves each of us that much. He is our Father. Let's not toss that term around lightly. God as our Father is a way of describing God as the most loving, caring Being in the universe. He created us and wants to have a close relationship with us. God not only made us in His image, the first thing He did after creating us was bless us and give us dominion over the earth.

Had Adam and Eve obeyed God, our picture of the Kingdom of God may have been very different because we may have been able to experience it in its fullness. Instead, we have only bits and pieces of the grand masterpiece that is the Kingdom. Thankfully, our Father is merciful. Rather than leaving us to fend for ourselves, God created an opportunity for us to be redeemed into right relations with Him by seeking His forgiveness (more on that later).

The aspect of the Kingdom this book seeks to address is the Community that God desires us to have. He has given us in the Bible a piece of literature that reveals some truths about Him so that we can experience His goodness on earth. When asked "What is the most important commandment?", Jesus replied,

> *"You must love the Lord your God with all your heart, all your soul, and all your mind. This is the first and greatest commandment. A second is equally important: 'Love your neighbor as yourself.'"*
> *Matt. 22:37*

Many Christians seem to have a decent grasp of the 'heart' and 'soul' parts of the command, but don't always consider what it means to love God with all our minds. While seeking knowledge rather than God is something we need to avoid, it's safe to say that Jesus wants us to use the intelligence that we have to discover as much about God as we can. That means, in part, studying the Bible and other Christian writings to see what truths God may be revealing in those words. When we do that, it can change what we thought it meant to love God with our minds, hearts, and souls, and how we see the world around us.

The Scriptures are an invitation for Creation to take part in an eternal Community with God as our loving ruler. It is filled with stories, songs, teachings, poems, and prophecies. It is a history, but it is not a textbook.

It is a love letter that is forever pointing us to Christ. It is all these things and so much more, and when we read the words we need to reflect on what the Scripture could be saying that may not be readily apparent, all the while realizing that we might not be correct in our interpretation. Jesus himself told His fellow Jews:

"You search the Scriptures because you think they give you eternal life. But the Scriptures point to me!"
John 5:39-40

The same is true of us. We come to the Scriptures and sometimes think we have done enough when, really, we need to come to the One who the words are talking about. Our chance at eternal life is only possible through Christ. We need to do more than just read the Bible, we need to become acquainted with the Person the Bible is about.

We can learn any number of things from the teachings of Christ, and something that is incredibly intriguing comes from His prayer for all believers. In John 17, we find this beautiful request from Christ on our behalf:

"I am praying not only for these disciples but also for all who will ever believe in me through their message. I pray that they will all be one, just as you and I are one − as you are in me, Father, and I am in you. And may they be in us so that the world will believe you sent me. I have given them the glory you gave me, so they may be one as we are one. I am in them and you are in me. May they experience perfect unity that the world will know that you sent me and that you love them as much as you love me."
John 17:20-23

This is the foundation on which we are going to expand. The Scriptures are not about us; they are about Christ. We are given the chance to find Christ and each other, for as Christ Himself prayed, He desires for us to find one another in this grand Community of believers. When we read the Bible, we are exploring an ancient text that is calling us to our Eternal Savior, who is encouraging us to engage with one another and walk through this life together.

When we see that truth, it becomes so important that we read the Bible to understand what it is telling us about Christ and see how it is describing the Kingdom. The Bible is powerful, and it is true; we just need to realize what that power and truth are telling us. It is not about you, and it's not about me. We need to stop reading the Bible with an egocentric inclination, and instead try to see what we can learn about Christ. When we do that, we begin to see that the Bible is about all of us. It is an eternal invitation to Community with God and by God, and this invitation can bring all of us together.

Since the Scriptures were written thousands of years ago, it's fair to assume that we will not be familiar with some ideas that would have been taken for granted when they were originally written. Consequently, we should always consider who wrote the passage, when and where they were writing, to whom they were writing, and what else was going on in the world at that time. A good place to start any Biblical study is by considering the context.

Verses In Context

INTRODUCTION

The Scriptures are an invitation for Creation to take part in an eternal Community that is consecrated by God. In order to see this aspect of the Scriptures, we should consider how God is introducing this eternal community and, at the same time, consider the historical background and significance of each passage. It is the reader's responsibility to consider what the text may have meant to its original readers by determining the author's place in society, the political and historical environment of the time, the location of the author as well as the intended audience, the general understanding of the text, and the purpose for its writing. This contextual criticism allows the reader to see the verse and how it relates to the big picture of Christianity.

Sprinkled throughout the book are fourteen brief Bible studies of verses that are very popular in American Christianity. These verses have been so popularized, in fact, that it seems as if they are often held above any sort of critical analysis. The meaning of these verses has been so widely accepted that their meaning is rarely questioned. It is possible that this is because the popular interpretation is right on the mark. But it is just as possible that we have been misunderstanding these verses for a long time. It is important to continue to review any passage, regardless of its popularity, so that we can continue to improve our understanding of Scripture. These readings are examples of contextual scriptural study, and they show how the popular interpretations of Scripture can be altered when we start to consider the 'who, what, when, where, and why' behind the text.

The verses we are going to study cover a range of topics, but they are all significant in that they are all extremely well-known, often memorized, and are used to address a myriad of circumstances. These studies will begin with a brief intro-duction of the verse's popular understanding, followed by an analysis of its context, and closing with a 'Connection' portion that offers a possible way of interpreting the passage that makes a connection between its historical significance and its meaning to the modern-day Christian. These are not meant to be extensive studies. In fact, much of the contextual analysis comes from simply reading the verses and chapters surrounding each verse to understand what else was going on. These are not the final answers of interpretation, but they are meant to take our level of Biblical scholarship one step further than we are used to. This is an introduction to genuine self-study and seeks to show what a difference intentional study can make in our lives as well as in the Kingdom.

Verses In Context Part I

JOSHUA 1:9

"This is my command — be strong and courageous! Do not be afraid or discouraged. For the Lord your God is with you wherever you go."

Joshua 1:9 often provides comfort to individuals facing difficult decisions or left with a general feeling of unease. You can find it on wall decorations and graduation cards and, if you grew up in church, you probably know the bible camp song as well. It's repeated so often that it's easy to minimize the power in these words. With that in mind, let's take a closer look at the background of Joshua 1:9.

CONTEXT

Chapter 1 of the book of Joshua opens "after the death of Moses" and begins with a couple of paragraphs of dialogue between the Lord and Joshua, who to this point in history has served as Moses' aide. In Joshua, we are transported to a time when the Israelites have lost their leader and are trying to figure out what to do next.

Joshua was anointed as Moses' successor in Numbers 27 and served as his aide until his passing in Deuteronomy 34. He was in favor of entering Canaan even when the rest of the nation was against it (Num. 13-14). He has seen some crazy things and has faithfully filled his role as Moses' sidekick for many years. Now, it is his time to lead the Israelites, and the Lord is telling him to prepare to enter the land He promised to them.

It seems a little odd that the Lord's instructions were centered on being strong and courageous when the land the Israelites were entering had been promised to them for generations. Why would they need any extra encouragement? We would expect that the nation would have been eager to walk into such a marvelous place, but Joshua realized that, even though the Lord had promised them safe passage, the Promised Land wasn't exactly free for the taking.

When Joshua and the Israelites arrived, the land of Canaan was inhabited by seven Canaanite tribes scattered all over the countryside (Joshua 3:10). As had happened throughout much of the Old Testament, the Israelites are promised by God that this land is theirs to invade, conquer, and claim as their own. What follows in the book of Joshua is the systematic takeover of all that the Lord had promised to the Israelites, but in chapter 1, we are still considering a people that is hesitant to even consider taking on seven other tribes.

According to the Lord's discourse with Joshua, God has promised the Israelites this land, and if the Canaanites remain in the land they will likely corrupt the Israelites. This corruption must not happen, so Joshua and his army must do everything that is necessary to rid the Promised Land of these unwanted, immoral, idolatrous neighbors.[10]

The irony of this story of Joshua and the Israelites is that it has already been told once before. About 40 years prior, when Moses was still leading the nation of Israel, Joshua himself was sent into Canaan as a spy to determine if the Israelites would be able to conquer the Promised Land. Unfortunately, when Joshua and his fellow spies returned and told their fellow Israelites that the Promised Land was already inhabited, he couldn't convince the rest of the people to continue with their plans to invade and take over the land of Canaan (Num. 13-14).

This initial lack of faith had a dreadful consequence, as God refused to allow any of the Israelites that were alive at the time, besides Joshua and Caleb (the only other spy who thought they should invade) to enter the Promised Land (Num. 14:26-35). This verdict was because the Israelites had not trusted God's ability to give them the land He had promised. Instead, the Israelites were forced to wander in the desert until Moses and the rest of the weak in faith had passed and Joshua had taken leadership (Deut. 3:21-22, 31:1-8).

So, in this first book of Joshua, we are seeing the culmination of 40 years of reparation because of the Israelites' disobedience. That much is true. But, we are seeing more than just a historical recitation, we are dealing with a book of theological history. In other words, this is not merely a chronological

---

10 "History Crash Course #14: Joshua and Conquest of the Promised Land," Aishcom, February 02, 2001, accessed February 14, 2018, www.aish.com/jl/h/cc/48932927.html

history that says, 'this is precisely what happened, when it happened, how it happened'. Rather, it is a depiction of an event with the purpose of teaching theological truths about God, man, sin, salvation, etc. It is not a simple recounting of events but is written with a goal in mind. It is supposed to teach us something, not just tell us what happened.[11] So, as we take the genre into account, it makes it even more important that we consider what the book is trying to show us about God as experienced by the ancient Israelites, rather than just taking it at the face value of 'this is what happened'.

As we make the connection, we need to engage with the Israelites as they have come to another crossroads and are forced to decide whether they will trust God or run away yet again.

CONNECTIONS

Joshua 1:9 shows the voice of the Lord encouraging Joshua, and all the Israelites, to believe Him when He makes a promise. This is the voice of the Almighty trying to urge His followers to head into battle, but it is also the voice of a loving Father trying to convince His children that they can trust in His promises. How ludicrous an idea that God's chosen people were unsure of the One in whom they should have been placing all their trust. But that was the case then, and it is often the case for many of us.

The Lord knows that what lies ahead of the Israelites is a

---

11 Bob Utley, "Introduction to Joshua," Bible.org, November 8, 2012, accessed February 14, 2018, bible.org/seriespage/introduction-joshua.

difficult and trying time of violence and that there will likely be times when they will feel as if the Lord has left them. Knowing this, the Lord is preemptively assuring His children of the love that will get them through those difficult times by promising to be with them "wherever they go."

Like many other verses, Joshua 1:9 is repeated so often that it can lose some of its power, but there is a lot more at stake here than a bad week, month, or even year. Instead of allowing our eyes to glaze over at the mention of Joshua and the Israelites, maybe we should ask the question, "Why is this verse repeated so much?"

It is repeated so much because it presents an immensely powerful truth that stretches throughout all of history. If we read the Bible straight through as it is written, then by the time we get to the story of Joshua we are reading about a people that have experienced God's fulfillment of His promises over and over. This is a multi-generational promise that is being tested yet again, and God is speaking to His children so lovingly that we should try to understand the context so that we can understand the depth of this love.

Here, God is saying that His promise still holds true despite years of trials, disobedience, and disbelief on the part of His chosen people. Rather than giving up on them, the Lord encourages them to "be strong and courageous", and to trust that He will be with them no matter where they go and what they face. That promise holds true to today's Christians as well.

That's exciting, but what can I do with it?

If we want to get the most out of a verse like Joshua 1:9, it's best to realize the fullness of the promise at hand, and not get hung up on the historical implications. God wants us to know that He will always be a source of strength to those who seek Him out. His promises are true for those who are taking an active part in His Kingdom. He wants everyone to be part of the eternal family, so that He can show Fatherly love to every one of His children. No matter what the situation, we have a Heavenly Father pushing us to get through it. God's promises do not expire like old milk, no matter how long it's been sitting out waiting to be used. You can always count on God to be there, and it's because of His presence that we do not have to be afraid.

PSALM 23

"The Lord is my shepherd; I have all that I need. He lets me rest in green meadows; he leads me beside peaceful streams. He renews my strength. He guides me along the right paths, bringing honor to his name. Even when I walk through the darkest valley, I will not be afraid, for you are close beside me. Your rod and your staff protect and comfort me. You prepare a feast for me in the presence of my enemies. You honor me by anointing my head with oil. My cup overflows with blessings. Surely your goodness and unfailing love will pursue me all the days of my life, and I will live in the house of the Lord forever."

Psalm 23 is a beautiful, poetic piece of Scripture that can be found on wall decorations, greeting cards, encouraging notes, and many other places in today's Christian culture. It's a chapter in a book in the middle of the Bible, surrounded by many other pieces of poetry, many of them written by David at various points during his life. But it is much more than a bit of literature that happens to roll off the tongue easily. It is a testimony to God's eternal glory evidenced in His love for all of us.

CONTEXT

It's hard to determine exactly when David wrote this Psalm. That makes it a little harder for us to completely understand the surroundings of the verse, but it's not as if David had any shortages of memorable experiences that are recorded in the

Bible. Let's look at who David is by considering some of his major life experiences.

David served as King of Israel, slayer of Goliath, redeemer of Jerusalem, father of King Solomon, and ancestor to Jesus Christ. Despite all these high points, David went through times of intense danger, dejection, and moral shortcomings.

It's important to remember that, while David did eventually defeat Goliath, he had to first muster up the courage to step on to the field of battle in the first place (1 Samuel 17). He became King of Israel, but his ascension to the throne was against great opposition from Saul, David's predecessor as King. Saul attempted to kill David on many occasions, and David was forced to flee and spend time in the wilderness to survive (1 Samuel 19-31).

Through these difficulties, David became one of the heroes of Christianity for his perseverance and willingness to serve the Lord through all his life. Even when he made mistakes and seemed to be straying from his faith, most infamously in his temptation and adultery in 2 Samuel 11, we see David as a man who was quite like many of us; he fell short of God's righteousness many times, but God remained faithful to His servant. His mistakes cannot be excused, but they should not keep us from perceiving David as a wonderful example of a servant of God.

Through these key points in David's life, we can come back to the realization that God continued to use him through these difficulties and missteps. In fact, it's easy to see a part of each of us in David's thoughts and actions. Not only is he a picture of Christ, but he is also a picture of each individual believer.

It's important to keep this in mind as we take a glance at the heart of David through his words in Psalm 23.[12]

When we read this Psalm, we are reading the words of one of the most influential and memorable figures in Scripture. To be even more specific, we are reading a praise song written as a poem. This is an expression of devotion and worship coming from a man of intense emotion. If we look at the rest of the Psalms, many of which were written by David, we can get a better idea of the emotional tendencies of the author. Psalm 23 is a praise of God's glory from one of God's children.

CONNECTION

David was a man who tended to be anxious about life. Many of the Psalms are echoes of a man pouring his heart out to God when he simply didn't know what else to do. In many ways, David is a lot like each of us. We can learn many lessons from his story and how we can deal with our own inclinations to anxiety.

In Psalm 23, David opens with a line that presents his situation in life as one of tranquility. The Lord is the One guiding his steps and keeping him from harm. Green pastures and still waters are sure to evoke feelings of peace in each of us, and David has a great affinity for the comfort he feels God has provided for him repeatedly.

Verse three, while still presenting a hopeful countenance, starts to turn toward something a little different. For David to

---

12 Stedman, Ray C.. 2 *Samuel: The Story of David*, Ray Stedman Ministries, www.pbc.org/files/584509049ad2b149c6f68278/0210.html

ascribe to God the power to "renew my strength" means that David has gone through times when his own power has not been enough, and he needed God to take over. David's very soul has, at some point, given up and required divine restoration. His restoration came through God, and David closes the stanza by returning to his description of God as leading him, this time to "bring honor to his name."

Then David becomes even more vulnerable to his reader, admitting to times when he has felt that he has walked "through the darkest valley." Since we don't know when David is writing this Psalm, we can't know for sure what experience he is referring to, but his wording makes it clear that he is speaking of times when his very life was at risk. And yet, he proclaims a freedom of fear that he has found in that same comfort he described in the beginning of the verse. His answer to fear and anxiety is to rest in God's leading him through his surroundings.

David closes Psalm 23 by saying God provided for him even when his enemies were nearby, and by affirming his faith in God to be present with goodness and mercy throughout his life. David's faith is evident in his proclamation that he will "live in the house of the Lord forever."

David's life, while spectacular in comparison to many of our lives, provides many examples for how to, and how not to, deal with anxiety and fear. In the case of Psalm 23, we need to learn from David that even when we find ourselves in the darkest of times, our comfort can be found in the One who is leading us everywhere we go.

When we look at this Psalm, and when we expand our view to the rest of the book, we see a litany of topics which we can deem worthy of bringing to God. Most of these works are aimed directly at God, and many are not nearly as pleasant as the 23rd. In fact, if we back up just one chapter and look at the opening of Psalm 22, we get a much different depiction of David as he says,

> *"My God, my God, why have you abandoned me? Why are you so far away when I groan for help? Every day I call to you, my God, but you do not answer. Every night I lift my voice, but I find no relief."*
> *Psalm 22:1-2*

The song ends on a much lighter note, but we can clearly see that David was not always as hopeful as he is in Psalm 23.

What can we do with this seemingly contradictory book?

We can see from the different genres within the book of Psalms that it is healthy for us to direct all our concerns toward God. It's difficult to break down and categorize every single Psalm into neat little boxes, but we can clearly see that within the book there are words of praise, lament, prophecy, tradition, and wisdom. That pretty much covers every aspect of our lives. It's easy to draw the conclusion that we should bring not only our excitement and joy, but also our anxieties and despair to God. We might not be able to handle our fluctuating emotions, but God certainly can. Psalm 23 is a perfect example of walking in the shadow of death, and yet experiencing comfort. When we are weighed down by our emotions, what better place to go than to God?

Our hope rests not in our own power to carry us through, but in the One who has promised to carry us. Psalm 23 is much more than a simple poem that looks nice when printed out, it is a fundamental promise from God being experienced by one of His followers. We can learn from David's ability to worship God despite finding himself in a dangerous place. In every big moment in his life, good or bad, David knew that his story was merely a portion of God's story, and it was God leading him throughout. His hope was found not in his own authority or achievements, but in the prospect of spending eternity in the house of the Lord. We should come to the same realization and place our hope in God's leading us through the story of the Kingdom.

JEREMIAH 29:11

"For I know the plans I have for you," says the Lord, "They are plans for good and not for disaster, to give you a future and a hope."

Jeremiah 29:11 is a go-to verse for many people experiencing a time of trouble or waiting without knowing what exactly they are waiting for. You can find it on greeting cards and wall decorations and keychains. It is so familiar now that it's easy to settle for its seemingly-obvious promise and miss the opportunity to dig deeper. It might make us feel good, but does the original context of the verse match up with the considerable number of situations for which it is used? Let's find out.

CONTEXT

A quick glance at Jeremiah 29 shows us that it is actually a letter written to "the exiles" of Babylon (v. 1-3). The Babylonians conquered the kingdom of Judah around 597 BCE and were forced to leave their homes and live in Babylon. There they lived in captivity until 538 BCE, when Persia conquered Babylon and said the Jews could return to their homeland.[13]

Already we can see that Jeremiah is not writing to an individual suffering some minor hardship, but to an entire nation that has been exiled and held captive in a foreign country. Understanding the audience's station in life gives us

---

13 "Babylonian Exile." *Encyclopædia Britannica*, Encyclopædia Britannica, Inc., www.britannica.com/event/Babylonian-Exile.

a better grasp at the intensity of the letter, but we also need to consider the author.

Jeremiah is a prophetic book, so it's easy to think that he is simply predicting the future, but he is doing much more than that. Jeremiah is speaking truth about the present and dealing with the mistakes of the past as well as predicting what may happen. His goal is extremely more diverse than simply for-tune-telling, and this can make the book seem disjointed or inconsistent at times. It's important that we consider his many goals when we study this book, and realize that his overarch-ing goal is to help his readers understand their role in God's Kingdom.

If you study Jeremiah 1, you'll see that Jeremiah is the son of Hilkiah, a priest, and that God called him to be one of his prophets. Before writing to the exiles, Jeremiah warned God's people that they were going to experience destruction because they had broken their covenant with God several times. Jeremiah's prophecy proved true when Babylon conquered the kingdom despite Jeremiah's warnings.[14] Despite their unwill-ingness to heed this previous advice, Jeremiah penned a letter of encouragement to the exiled nation, and that's where we find chapter 29.

CONNECTION

Jeremiah 29:11 holds a truth that is much more complex and

---

14 Moen, Chris. "Jeremiah the Prophet." *Life, Hope & Truth,*. life-hopeandtruth.com/prophecy/prophets/prophets-of-the-bible/jeremiah-the-prophet/

meaningful than some of the trivial difficulties to which we typically relate it. That doesn't mean it is irrelevant to our present situation, it just means that we need to take a different approach to understanding its meaning.

God makes a lot of promises throughout the Bible, and as Christians we are heirs to those promises, and they hold true for all eternity. That doesn't necessarily mean that every promise to every person in the Bible is meant to apply to every person in every situation throughout history. In this case, God is promising the Jews that they will experience freedom again, even though it might not happen the way they are expecting. If we keep reading, we see that God was faithful to his promise and the exiled Jews were given the freedom to return to their homeland.

God made a promise, through Jeremiah, and He kept His promise.

So, what can we take from this verse in our lives today?

We see that this promise is meant for a community as well as individuals. After all, without the individual there would be no community. God's promise to the Jews provided a hope for future redemption into right relationship with God, and that promise can mean the same thing to all people in all times. That's the promise we should be focusing on here. This isn't a promise that is meant to say that everything will work out for your own personal benefit, it's a promise that says it will work out for the good of the Kingdom.

We can be sure that God is working to redeem all of Creation to Himself. When we don't know the plans God has for each of us individually, we can read Jeremiah's letter and find that

God's plan has never been about just one person, but has always been about the whole community. [15]

It's easy to think the Bible is only speaking to us because there's so many questions we need answered, but the promise God is making is much, much bigger than our individual lives, and that should give us even more hope. God provides a hope for individuals as well as entire nations at the same time. Jeremiah 29:11 is not just a quick fix for when you're feeling lost and confused, it's a reminder that we are all part of a much greater plan than we could ever imagine.

---

15 "Stop Taking Jeremiah 29:11 Out of Context." *RELEVANT Magazine,* 7 June 2017, relevantmagazine.com/god/practical-faith/stop-taking-jeremiah-2911-out-context. Accessed 23 Aug. 2017.

PHILIPPIANS 4:13

"For I can do everything through Christ, who gives me strength."

Philippians 4:13 is a verse that is often used to inspire young people when they are trying to decide what they want to be in the world. It is quoted to get people to believe in themselves and be confident that they are capable of much more than they can imagine through the strength of God. It's on keychains, coffee mugs, t-shirts, cell phone cases, and tattooed on numerous professional athletes. It can be used as an inspiration for winning the big game or dreaming of a better life, but let's try to figure out what Paul might have had in mind when he wrote this letter to the church in Philippi.

CONTEXT

Paul wrote this letter after visiting the church in Philippi, so he knew some of the people there and was at least somewhat familiar with their struggles as well as their strengths. He is writing to address those things, as well as to let them know how things are in prison – Paul spent some time in a Roman jail for his relentless sharing of the faith. He wrote several of his letters while imprisoned, and Philippians is one of them. [16]

---

16   Herrick, Greg. "Introduction, Background, and Outline to Philippians." *Bible.org*, bible.org/seriespage/introduction-background-and-outline-philippians/.

Paul's environment when he wrote Philippians 4:13 is a clue that the sense of invincibility which the verse is sometimes used to evoke was probably not what Paul had in mind at all. It would be hard to feel invincible while sitting in a first-century jail cell, so why would Paul attempt to convince his readers that he could do whatever he wanted. He was probably having a tough time beating the rats to his daily meal rations, so forget about doing "everything." Paul is not simply telling the Christians in Philippi to dream bigger dreams or that they can do whatever they want because they have God on their side. Look at verses 11 and 12. Paul is telling them that even though he is sitting in a dirty, stinking jail cell, he is content. There's nothing to do with superhuman feats of strength or changing the world or anything like that.

In fact, some versions of the Bible even have a slightly different wording that make it clear what Paul is talking about. The New King James Version, for example, does not quote Paul saying he can do all "things" but instead says all "this." That version might not roll of the tongue quite as easily, and it doesn't sound quite as motivating, but it makes it a whole lot easier to see that Paul is talking about something different than what most Christians probably expect.

CONNECTION

Paul is telling Christians, in a way, that they can do all things through Christ, but he's thinking of things like surviving in a disease-infested prison. He's teaching us that we can get through even the most difficult times because God is there to strengthen us. Paul is saying that Christians are invincible, it's just that we're not invincible in the way we might be picturing.

Then what way is he talking about?

Philippians 4:13 is one of the most encouraging verses in the Bible, we just need to figure out what exactly it is encouraging us to do. Instead of using this verse as a pump-up speech to conquer the world, we need to use it as a pick-me-up when we're feeling like we have nothing left. Paul isn't teaching us to be superheroes, he's telling us that by focusing on the hope and strength that Jesus gives us through the Holy Spirit, we can pull through the darkest of days.

"What was that about superheroes?"

Remember in *The Dark Knight Rises* when Bruce Wayne ends up imprisoned in what is basically a giant pit full of some hard-core criminals? He's stuck. There's almost no hope of him getting out alive. Sounds kind of like Paul sitting in a Roman jail, doesn't it?

Now, Paul and Bruce Wayne are far the same, but there are some similarities. Both men were faced with a seemingly hopeless situation, and they both could easily have given up. But they didn't. They stayed strong in the face of overwhelming odds and overcame their difficulties.

In Bruce Wayne's case, he built up his strength and was eventually able to make a seemingly impossible escape so that he could go be Batman and save Gotham from destruction. In Paul's case, he was content right where he was because he knew that, one way or another, he would be released from his imprisonment and would be able to rejoice with God in his freedom.

Okay, so what does that mean?

I think we need to take a cue from both Paul and Bruce Wayne. Even when we find ourselves stuck in a dark place, feeling like there's no way out, we can't give up our hope in the strength of God to pull us through.

Philippians 4:13 is about getting through the hard times by relying on God's strength, not about throwing the winning touchdown pass at the Super Bowl.

After all, only two people in the world get to play quarterback in the Super Bowl each year, but everyone will go through some dark times in life. God's promise is, again, far bigger than we could ever imagine. When you consider that this is a promise to all people, it's an astonishing thought that we can "do all things through Christ…"

How Scripture Divides

It is interesting and disturbing to think that the book around which Christians should be finding the most common ground is cause for vehement disputes and fracturing of relationships within the Church. Though opportunities for disagreement and division are plenty, God's call on our lives is one of unity amidst disunity, and identity in community. To avoid these disagreements and create an environment of belonging, it's important that we explore how reading the same text can result in so many different interpretations.

Once we engage with the difficulties of Scripture, we can move forward in such a way as to improve our relationships with each other and allow for grace to work its way into our lives. We need to remember that our personal interpretation of Scripture is certainly not the only one, and that our goal should never be to be right, but to build on our relationship with God and with the Kingdom.

In 2 Timothy 3:16, Timothy gives us an introduction to the Bible when he tells us that;

"All Scripture is inspired by God and is useful to teach us what is true and to make us realize what is wrong in our lives. it corrects us when we are wrong and teaches us to do what is right."

That would be a good one-liner to use for the back cover. From Timothy's introduction, we should realize that since Scripture is "inspired by God", that probably means we need to take it seriously. Not only that, but we need to be careful when we discuss what it means. It is meant to be used in a variety of ways, and that could drastically alter how we interpret a singular verse. It's dangerous to assume that we know just as much as God and that a cursory reading of the Gospel is all that is required to understand it. For us to be responsible participants, we need to come to Scripture humbly and faithfully ready to learn all that we can from the wisdom God has revealed to us. What we are dealing with is God's revelation of Himself to His children. We are here to learn, not to impose our preconceptions on the text.

We are called to have faith and trust in God. But what exactly is faith? We can start by saying that faith is, in part, an admittance that God knows more than we know. If we knew everything that God knew, what would be the point of entrusting our care to Him? Therefore, if we admit that God knows more than our minds can ever comprehend, then it makes sense that any word that has been inspired by Him likely holds more meaning than can be gathered with a quick reading.

This doesn't mean that God is trying to trick us by hiding what He really means. Many verses are so simple that it would be harder for us to make up another meaning than the one right in front of us. But God's infinite wisdom does mean that we have to make sure that what we understand to be true is what God is really trying to tell us. God knows more than we do, and the Bible is a chance for us to glimpse at the mind of God and see what He is telling us.

It then follows that to discuss the Bible is also an act of faith. It is an act of humility to admit that reading is not enough, and that there is more to the text than can be understood at first glance. The Bible is a book of infinite wisdom and requires committed investigation. Anyone can turn to a random page, read a verse or two, and declare their all-knowing wisdom of what that passage means and how it relates to them and to the Kingdom. However, it takes humility to sacrifice our time and energy to explore the possibilities of the Scriptures. Probing each verse is an admittance that there might be more to it than you realized. It is worth our time and effort because we are seeking the face of God. Unfortunately, no amount of time guarantees that we will know exactly what the Bible is telling us every time.

This further complicates the process, as any amount of time spent studying the Scripture may not be enough. We likely will never know the purpose of some verses found in the Bible. Only God knows why the book was written the way it was written, for the Scripture is 'God-breathed'. If you don't believe me, take a stroll through some books like Daniel, Song of Songs, Judges, or maybe Revelation. These books and many others are true and good for us to engage with, but that does not mean they are easy to understand. Humans may have written the words and determined what could be considered sacred and included in the Word, but these words are still the result of God's work in His servants and need to be given due respect and diligence in our interpretation. With that said, we also need to be content with not being able to grasp everything that the Bible says. This contentment can lead to some amazing things.

One of the most beautiful aspects of Christianity is that not everyone will agree on how to interpret the Bible. This may seem like a setback, but this flexibility in explaining Scripture allows for more growth to come from discussing its meaning. The communal aspect of the faith is made more realistic by healthy conversation, and differing interpretations allow for these conversations to be more common.

It is important that these are discussions rather than arguments. Arguments are deconstructive, whereas discussions are constructive. It is not our responsibility to be right, but to admit our frailty by lowering our sense of superiority to exchange ideas with another person. The Bible is not something that is meant to divide its audience, but it is meant to instruct, correct, and to be discussed in a healthy manner. It is not a problem to be solved, it is a message to be proclaimed.

Yet, the Church misses the mark on the call to unity far too often. Let's talk about why the Bible is the source of such division among the very people who claim to hold it as the most sacred text.

BIBLE BATTLES

The Bible is debated so much simply because of its communal nature and because of the power in its words. There have been generations of Bible readers and consequently, generations of people discussing its meaning. What we are reading in the Bible is a collection of books that were compiled and deemed sacred by generations of scholars over hundreds of years. It did not pass directly from God to us. It has gone through intense scrutiny since it was written, and all we are doing is providing new interpretations, or recounting old interpretations that are simply new to us.

Reading the Bible as an invitation to Community bares the reality that it is a book of change. We have trouble reconciling the contradictions the Bible makes with itself because we fail to realize that it is a book that is depicting thousands of years of history. A lot happens in that time, including a change in how the people of that time thought about and tried to understand God.

Furthermore, within that history we are often dealing with texts that were not necessarily written to be taken literally. Much of the Old Testament is written as theological history, meant to provide a glimpse into God's purpose without relaying actual historical facts. Some problems in interpretation occur when we read Scripture as a historical textbook even though it was not written that way. None of this makes the Bible any less important. The Bible is paramount to our faith because every book is moving us toward God's offer of redemption. We just might not always know exactly how it is doing so.

There is a chance that some of the more difficult books (specifically, some of the books of the Old Testament that depict a nation of Israel that is bent on war and destruction as the main method of gaining God's favor) are simply meant to show us that our Christian ancestors had a different perception of God. We need to remember the Old Testament is an ancient text attempting to explain God's work in the world at that time. We should also consider that the Old Testament is about individuals who did not know or fully understand the coming Messiah because He was just that – still coming. We are moving through church history as we move through the Bible which means we are seeing different styles of interpretation.

That doesn't mean that the Old Testament is any less useful than the New Testament, it just means that we have to read those books differently. Reading the books of the Old Testament on their own can't bring anyone to Christ, but reading the Old Testament Christian-ly can. That is, reading the Old Testament with the knowledge of who Christ is and how He allows for redemption can help us encounter the stories of Exodus, the lamentations of Ecclesiastes, the dismay of Job, the contradictions of Psalms, and all the Old Testament in a way that informs our understanding of how Christ affected the world.

The Bible is a book that depicts a community that has changed throughout its history. Yet, it is not a science nor history textbook. It is difficult to make any concrete claims at the science of the natural world or how God wants us to act based simply on history. Much of the Old Testament depicts a God who encouraged the nation of Israel to commit genocide on the surrounding peoples. The medieval Church also rejected the scientific theory that the earth revolved around the sun because of how they interpreted the Bible. Does that make these groups completely wrong? Or was the Bible wrong?

Maybe neither the Bible nor the people were wrong. Maybe it was simply a misunderstanding of what God is trying to tell us. It's safe to say that God is not trying to explain the way the world works scientifically, there just is not enough concrete information for that. It also doesn't mean that He is trying to give us a day-by-day history that shows us exactly what happened and when it happened. There are too many contradictions and inconsistencies to back that up. No, the Bible is trying to show us a glimpse of the face of God. If we read it any other way, it simply does not make much sense. The Bible is about the Kingdom, and the Kingdom is about God.

In many Biblical battles, the final answer is that there is no final answer. The vast number of possible interpretations means that sometimes we simply cannot know the answer to life's most complex questions because the Bible itself is complex. It doesn't give easy answers to complex questions. If it did, then the work of faith in our lives would be much less necessary for us to come to know Christ. Our trust should be in God, not in the Bible. The Bible is one of God's ways of revealing Himself to Creation, but if we could understand God fully through the Bible, then we would no longer need a relationship with Him. The Bible is the most direct way for us to seek God's face, but to do so as a true Community, we need to make room for even the most opposing interpretations to exist alongside one another.

Allowing for different interpretations leads to a more complete Kingdom because we can allow more room for grace to work as we extend the invitation. It's as simple as that. We can't exclude anyone based on their opinion unless that opinion detracts from what we know God to be. How can we be sure of the nature of God? We can know God through the person of Jesus Christ, that is the beauty of the Incarnation. Christ is the example of God through whom we can perceive righteousness. Therefore, we can turn to the example of Jesus whenever we are faced with differing opinions. It is not always a clear-cut determination, but Christ is the final word, and through Him we can see that the grace of God is an invitation that extends to everyone – people from every race, religious background, economic situation, or any other determining factor of status in society.

Our faith is not based on theological or intellectual debate but on relationships and on changed lives that exist because of the connections that are available through the discussion of Scripture. The problem of Scripture contradicting itself can be handled if we accept our fallibility and allow grace to work in our churches. The nuances of Scripture provide another invitation to community because they allow for people of differing opinions to coexist.

What we need to realize is that our unity doesn't come from standing together on every belief but admitting that we are all broken in the same way, and we are all incapable of comprehending our Father in His magnificence. As in any family, we will have disagreements, but that doesn't mean we can say we are no longer part of the same family. The Kingdom of God is eternal, no one gets to leave just because their beliefs are not the exact same as another member of the Kingdom.

With that said, the only way we cannot coexist with differing beliefs is when those beliefs shake the very foundation of our understanding of who God is. Any interpretation that seeks to portray God as evil, limited, imperfect, unjust, or anything apart from what we can determine God is through perceiving the person of Jesus Christ did not come from a healthy place. But if the interpretation in question does not detract from the holy perfection of God, then it is an interpretation worth considering. Now of course, we need to draw a line somewhere to keep this open mindset from leading us astray. Therefore, we need to realize that there are some essentials to Christianity, things like the belief in the Trinity, the divinity and humanity of Jesus, the Crucifixion and Resurrection, and the opportunity for Salvation. But the work of grace in the Christian faith is shown in the need to allow some breathing room when it comes to beliefs that are not essential.

BUT WHAT IF I'M WRONG?

My interpretation of Scripture will never be completely 'right', and I am more than okay with it. You don't have to agree with anything I've said because what I've said is based on my interpretation of faith that comes from my contextual experience with God. But you see, that's just the point – even if you disagree, we can still engage in a healthy conversation that can explore the possibilities that lie in the mysterious majesty of the Creator. Being 'right' about every little detail is not the most important thing, the most important thing is the love of God.

I find it very hard to believe God would keep someone out of Heaven because they were baptized by sprinkling instead of immersion, or because they believed the earth wasn't created in six literal days. Maybe that's just me, but I believe God is far more gracious than we give Him credit for. We cannot determine who gets into Heaven, but if we send another person out of our lives because some of their beliefs are different, I think we are running too high of a risk of turning them completely away from faith. We will not make the final judgment, but we can have a great effect on one another's path to eternity. It is not our role to play judge nor jury, but to offer the same kind of love we want others to offer to us.

Everything comes down to love. Not a superficial love, but a love that looks past differences and sees another heart yearning for the same experience of the Father. If we are trying to follow the example of Christ, we need to be striving for an *'agape'* love – a love that is unconditional and always seeks the good of the whole rather than the good of the individual. God is love, love is truth, and truth is anything that moves us toward God[17]. Every person is our neighbor and is worthy of love and acceptance. Or better yet, every person is just as unworthy of love as we are, so who are we to withhold our hearts from welcoming another broken creature into the family of God? There's nothing easy about loving each other in the way that God loves us, but it is vital that we do.

---

17 The Liturgists. (2014). *Episode 4 - Church Unity*. [podcast] Available at: http://www.theliturgists.com/podcast/?offset=1414468860000 [Accessed 28 Oct. 2017].

Responsible Participants

These first couple of verses, and the dozen that follow, are all examples of how Scripture presents the Kingdom of God to all of Creation. For the time being, let's accept that we are all participating in this Kingdom in some way or another, whether we are aware of our participation or not. So instead of asking if we can be part of 'something bigger', let's ask how we can be effective, responsible participants in the eternal Community of God. How does God desire us to play our roles in His masterpiece?

RESPONSIBLE PARTICIPANTS

To be responsible participants is to be responsible Christians. That is, we need to follow the teachings and instructions of God through Christ to learn what it means to be a Child of God. Our salvation is by faith – that is true, but if that is where we stop the conversation then we are forgetting the actions that must flow out of our faith. True salvation must result in a completely changed person, and that includes how they act in relation to the world around them. This means that the responsibility acquired through salvation is one of changed motives that results from certain active decisions.

BELONG, BEHAVE, BELIEVE

These active decisions can be labeled as actions of belonging, of behavior, and of belief. In many churches, the qualification for church membership begins with believing the right things, which leads to behaving the right way. Only once the belief and behavior are present can a person really be accepted as an active participant in the congregation. However, that doesn't really seem to be the timeline that we should be following. In fact, if we look at Jesus' willingness to seek out the undesirable and invite them into His presence, fully aware that they did not know the One to whom they were speaking, we might consider that our model should be flipped.

To actively seek out new believers, we should be creating a sense of belonging first. Through our study in Scripture, we are seeing that all of humanity is already a part of the Kingdom. That means that every person that walks through the doors of the church automatically belongs as an active member of the congregation. If we are all part of the same eternal Kingdom, then no matter how many times you split up the larger group into smaller congregations, every member should be able to feel that they belong.

If we look at the example Jesus gave for us, we can see that actions of genuine love and acceptance should be our response to anyone we meet. Christ made no conditions on who He spent His time with; His friends were tax collectors, prostitutes, and adulterers. In fact, the Gospels make no mention of whether these individuals were even interested in the message of the

Son of God, but Jesus loved them and treated them like family no matter what their perception of Him. Our churches should function the same way. We should be welcoming in everyone, because every person needs a family to love on them. It would be wrong of us to stay inside the safety of our little circle and exclude any newcomer on whatever basis or anxiety we may have. The way to the Kingdom is an open door through a heart of genuine love and acceptance.

Once we have established a feeling of love and acceptance, we need to realize that our time is more valuable than we think it is. What I'm saying is that Jesus didn't come just to spend time with people; He came to heal people. In the same way, our lives should be focused on healing the hurt of those around us. The best way to create an environment in which everyone feels that they belong is to admit our own brokenness and allow healing to take place in our lives. Admitting our own vulnerability is the only way to build authentic relationships that can lead to mutual healing.

Openness and intimacy are some behaviors that should be present in any healthy relationship. The only way to create enough safety to be able to have times of vulnerability is by making sure everyone knows that they belong and that all are broken, then behaviors like small group bible studies, baptismal services, communion, and even the post-service meet-and-greet become like food to the hungry. These opportunities to actively affirm our commitment to God, as a body of believers, is vital to allow each person to examine their beliefs, which is what it is all really about.

As the behavior permeates in each life that is present, the

beliefs start to unfold and lead to a greater understanding of what Christianity is all about. The sense of community has already been established, and that creates a safety net for each member to examine their personal beliefs and compare them to the beliefs of the congregation. A safe environment allows each member to grow at their own pace without feeling like they will be left behind. This way, every member can recognize their place as a valued member of the church which they attend as well as the universal Church. They can then participate in the life of the Kingdom by continually inspecting the doctrines and beliefs of their congregation to create an even greater foundation for community.

The goal then becomes one geared toward the betterment of the whole, and makes it less likely that anyone should try to earn salvation selfishly. Scriptural study should create a desire to examine the actions of the group to ensure that the entire group is living righteously. It is important that we realize that a desire for communal health means we should also be examining ourselves, because an individual's personal health greatly influences that of the whole.

Once the behaviors begin to feel more natural, each member of the group can begin examining their personal beliefs as well as the stated beliefs of the congregation, denomination, etc. We should constantly examine our own beliefs to avoid overlooking any big points. Any time there is a large group of people adhering to one sacred text, the result is a mish-mash of differing opinions about that text. We can see evidence of this in any number of religions as well as political ideologies. Christians should seek a different path to unity. It is only by belonging and seeking to behave as a group that we can safely evaluate our beliefs to ensure a safe, strong, Community of God-seekers.

It's important to not get too hung up on this idea and treat it like a step-by-step process on the way to righteousness. It is not. This 'belong, behave, believe' mantra is merely seeking to turn our hearts toward loving each other as Jesus loves us. We would never say that Jesus does not make Himself available to every person, no matter what they may be struggling with. So why should we be the ones to make the judgment on who can and cannot participate in our community? Jesus loved every person He met. It's as simple as that. Obviously that doesn't mean we should allow someone to intentionally destroy the church, but all are welcome that are genuinely searching.

It may seem like a backward idea to anyone that hasn't heard it before, but I hope that it strikes a compassionate chord in your heart. When Jesus told us to love one another, He never said to only love those who are like us, or who are trying to be like us. He simply said to love. Without qualification, condition, or requirement. So how do we love? Well, we can start by extending the grace of God to each person we come across, not only in church on Sunday mornings, but also in the grocery store on Tuesday afternoon, the basketball game Friday night, at work on Monday morning; you get the picture.

"But we must draw the line somewhere, right? We can't just let everyone have a say."

Are you sure we need to draw a line? If I remember right, Jesus drew a line once.

"but early the next morning he was back again at the Temple. A crowd soon gathered, and he sat down and taught them. As he was speaking, the teachers of religious law and the Pharisees brought a woman who had been caught in the act of adultery. They put her in front of the crowd.

"Teacher," they said to Jesus, "this woman was caught in the act of adultery. The law of Moses says to stone her. What do you say?" They were trying to trap him into saying something they could use against him, but Jesus stooped down and wrote in the dust with his finger. They kept demanding an answer, so he stood up again and said, "All right, but let the one who has never sinned throw the first stone!" Then he stooped down again and wrote in the dust.

When the accusers heard this, they slipped away one by one, beginning with the oldest, until only Jesus was left in the middle of the crowd with the woman. Then Jesus stood up again and said to the woman, "Where are your accusers? Didn't even one of them condemn you?"

"No, Lord," she said.

And Jesus said, "Neither do I. Go and sin no more."

John 8:2-11

Maybe, just maybe, what Jesus wants us to do is much simpler than we have made it out to be. None of this means it will always be easy to welcome new members to our community. "What about that time they said something mean about you? Did you hear what he did last week?" But we can't ignore Jesus' warning against condemning one another. Love and acceptance may not always be easy, but it can be incredibly simple. Love each other despite our wrongdoing. Welcome each other to a community of people that just want to support each other. That is the only way we can hope to become something like the Community which we all desire.

If we honestly love each other, we can become a community that gives back to itself rather than one that requires certain qualifications before any new member can participate. The Kingdom of God is an invitation, not a job application. We are qualified to actively participate in the narrative of Creation simply by being alive. It's not our place to determine who is in and who is out. It is merely our responsibility to walk alongside each other in our brokenness and prayerfully hope that we can help one another become more like Christ.

WHY IS IT SO HARD TO AGREE?

Many of the most intense disagreements in Christianity center around differing interpretations of Scripture. It is interesting to think that the book around which Christians should be finding the most common ground is cause for vehement disputes and fracturing of relationships within the Church. Though opportunities for disagreement and division are plenty, God's call on our lives is one of unity amidst disunity, and identity in community. To avoid these disagreements and create an environment of belonging, it's important that we explore how reading the same text can result in so many different interpretations. Once we engage with the problem of Scripture, we can move forward in such a way as to improve our standing with each other and allow for grace to work its way into our lives. We need to remember that our personal interpretation of Scripture may not be the best one, and furthermore, that our goal should never be to be right, but to build on our relationship with God and with the Kingdom.

Verses In Context Part II

ISAIAH 40:31

"But those who trust in the Lord will find new strength.
They will soar high on wings like eagles.
They will run and not grow weary.
They will walk and not faint."

Remember The Titans, the 2000 film depicting a high school football team from Virginia which overcame racial tensions and segregation on their way to a state championship, includes a memorable scene in which the football team calls a players-only meeting in the high school gym that ends in a raucous recitation of this verse from Isaiah. If you haven't had the pleasure of watching the film, chances are you have probably seen this verse pop up somewhere else in your life as an encouragement to someone either going through a difficult time or facing a challenge that has them concerned. It's a verse that is often paired with athletic challenges because of its wording, but what did the prophet Isaiah have in mind?

CONTEXT

One of the biggest questions we need to answer is who wrote chapter 40 of the book of Isaiah? Traditionally, the prophet Isaiah has been given credit for the entire book. However, that assumption has come under some scrutiny by many biblical scholars because chapters 40-55 are very different from the first 39 chapters of the book.

The first section of the book is mostly Isaiah bringing the word of God to Judah and the nations around Judah. But then, in chapter 40, the time switches to after the destruction of Jerusalem and the author is clearly addressing the Jews while they are exiled in Babylon.

All of this is important because Isaiah lived from about 760 to 700 B.C. Most of his writing fits this timeline. However, the destruction of Jerusalem did not happen until more than 100 years after Isaiah died. To make things even more confusing, chapters 56-55 of Isaiah seem to be written after the exiles have returned home, which didn't happen for another 70 years after the destruction of Jerusalem. Basically, it doesn't make sense that Isaiah would be addressing an event that happened long after his death when most of his writing seems to address things that would have been relevant during his life. It is possible that God could have revealed 150 years of future affairs to Isaiah so that he could write the last half of his book – he was a prophet after all – but we can't say that is what happened without a doubt. [18]

---

18 "Bible Gateway." III. *Structure, Authorship, And Date of Isaiah - Asbury Bible Commentary - Bible Gateway*, www.biblegateway.com/resources/ asbury-bible-commentary/Structure-Authorship-Date.

Okay, then what do we know?

No matter who the author of this verse is, it is obvious that he is writing to a group of people in exile. They have been removed from their homeland and forced to live in a foreign country. The Jews have been forced to leave Judah and are living under Babylonian jurisdiction. While you could say that this is just because of the aggression of the Babylonians, the author places all the blame on the Jews for their disobedience and disrespect toward God.

It is also a fair assumption that, like much of Isaiah, we are reading Hebrew poetry that is meant to intrigue the reader and share a truth of God. It is a theological, rather than historical, work of worship that depicts the author's understanding of God. It is supposed to be enlightening to the readers and share a theological truth relevant to the historical and religious situation of the time.

Despite the guilt of the Jews in their unfortunate situation, chapter 40 of Isaiah is a chapter of encouragement rather than condemnation. The author tells the readers that trusting in God will help them get through even the most hopeless times in life. This is where we find Isaiah 40:31.

CONNECTION

It's easy to lose the overwhelming power of this verse by simply repeating it to the point that it is little more than words on a page, but if we do that we are forgetting just how meaningful these words would have been to the original readers. Imagine if you were in the situation that the Kingdom of Judah is in at this point in history. The Temple of Jerusalem, easily the most important structure for the Jews and a visible sign of the power of God, has been destroyed and the people were exiled from their homeland and forced to live in Babylon.

It is in this hopeless situation that we find the Kingdom of Judah. And then they hear these words from Isaiah, telling them to hope in the Lord. Some of us might find that to be too simple of an answer in such a dark time, but for these people, in this time, this could have been the glimmer of hope they had been waiting for.

After years of disobeying God and refusing to heed warnings from prophets like Isaiah, the Jews are still given another chance to come back to God. This is like God saying, "we both know you've been unfaithful in this relationship, but I'm still willing to hold up my end of the bargain. If you'll just come back to me, I can help you get through this."

This is where we need to consider what difference it makes that Isaiah is a work of prophetic literature. Prophecy is not fortune telling, it is actually far more reflective than we sometimes realize. Often, prophecy is used to remind the people of Israel of their history. Throughout the Old Testament we see five major promises from God to His people. It is these covenants that most prophetic literature has in mind when the authors call their audience back to obedience.

In Genesis 9:11, God establishes a covenant with Noah that, "Never again will floodwaters kill all living creatures; never again will a flood destroy the earth."" Then, God promises Abram in Genesis 12, "I will make you into a great nation. I will bless you and make you famous, and you will be a blessing to others." This covenant is more conditional, as it requires

Abram's obedience. The third major covenant comes in Exodus 19, when God tells the nation of Israel, through Moses, "Now if you will obey me and keep my covenant, you will be my own special treasure from among all the peoples on earth; for all the earth belongs to me." After the people broke their end of this bargain, God reestablishes a covenant in 2 Samuel 7, when He spoke to King David through His prophet, Nathan: "I will provide a homeland for my people Israel, planting them in a secure place where they will never be disturbed. Evil nations won't oppress them as they've done in the past." It is in this covenant that God goes on to promise an eternal Kingdom, that will ultimately be fulfilled in Christ. The final covenant we will look at comes in Jeremiah 31 when, despite continual disobedience on the part of the people of God, the Father graciously establishes a New Covenant by saying, "This is the new covenant I will make with the people of Israel after those days. I will put my instructions deep within them, and I will write them on their hearts. I will be their God, and they will be my people."

"With all those covenants, how do we know which one Isaiah is addressing?"

It just takes a brief glimpse at the table of contents to reasonably rule out the New Covenant found in Jeremiah, because that came after Isaiah's time. It makes sense that Isaiah is calling to mind the most recent covenant to his time, the one that his audience would be most familiar with, and that is the Davidic Covenant which we find in 2 Samuel. There, God promises to provide a place for His people. This is imme-diately relatable to a people in exile! Isaiah is re-presenting this promise of safety at a time when his audience desperately needs a source of hope. This is an incredible reminder that their story isn't over, and that God has promised to help them through this difficult time.

"Why would God do such a thing?"

Because God's promises are eternal. That promise is the same today as it was thousands of years ago. If we can place our hope in God no matter what is going on around us, God is able and willing to strengthen us. It sounds simple, but once you experience that divine strength, it is unmistakable and even addicting. Just like the author is encouraging the Jews, the Lord can renew our strength and make us feel like we are flying above the clouds. We may grow physically tired, but our spiritual energy will never run out so long as we continue to stay close to God and place our hope in Him alone.

MATTHEW 11:30

"For my yoke is easy to bear, and the burden I give you is light."

Jesus makes many promises to His followers throughout the Gospels, so it's easy to overlook similar statements as mere re-presentations of the same ideas. Matthew 11:30 is one such statement that we could just glance at and move on, but that might be neglecting a key lesson from Christ. Is He bragging to us that His life is easy? Is He saying that our lives will be easy if we follow Him? Or is He saying something else entirely?

CONTEXT

Jesus' teaching in Matthew 11 comes in the early stages of His ministry. He had just appointed apostles to go to the "God's lost sheep" and begin performing miracles and teaching the truth they have found in Christ. Jesus gave them numerous instructions as well as the authority to drive out evil spirits and heal disease and sickness. After He sent out the twelve, Jesus went to the towns of Galilee to preach to the people there.

It is in Galilee that Jesus is confronted by the disciples of John the Baptist, who is imprisoned at the time, and asked whether He is the Messiah. Jesus' response, while not direct, affirms that He is the One they have been waiting for, the Savior. After Jesus identifies Himself as such, He begins to speak to the crowd about John's greatness, saying, "of all who have ever lived, none is greater than John the Baptist."

After praising John, Jesus takes a different tone and begins to address the cities in which He performed most of His miracles. These cities, despite having seen Christ's power, remained unrepentant and so, Jesus began to denounce these places and warn that they will experience a terrible day of judgment because of their unrepentant spirit.

At the end of chapter 11, Christ changes His tone from judgment to redemption, and this is where we find our verse in question. Christ begins this section by praising the Father for hiding things from the wise and revealing them to little children. He speaks of His close relationship with the Father, saying, "No one truly knows the Son except the Father, and no one truly knows the Father except the Son and those to whom the Son chooses to reveal him." Then Jesus leaves His audience with an invitation. He tells His listeners,

> *"Come to me, all of you who are weary and carry heavy burdens, and I will give you rest. Take my yoke upon you. Let me teach you, because I am humble and gentle at heart, and you will find rest for your souls. For my yoke is easy to bear, and the burden I give you is light."*

CONNECTION

As we expand our view beyond the final verse of the chapter, we see that what we are reading is more than a description of the state of affairs in Jesus' life or our own lives. Rather, this is an invitation to come to Jesus for rest and strength. Christ is giving us the opportunity to experience the help that comes with giving our burdens to Him.

Instead of trying to do things with our own strength, Jesus

is inviting us to come to Him. Note that the way we can come to enjoy the rest and ease that comes from Him is by learning from Him. Specifically, Christ wants to teach us gentleness and humility, for these characteristics can help us with our burdens.

Think about that for a second, and you will realize that Jesus isn't exactly saying that if we choose to follow His teachings everything will automatically get easier. We might have a mental picture of Jesus reaching down and picking the heavy weight off our backs and allowing us to walk on unencumbered by whatever was previously giving us trouble. But that's not really what He's saying.

"What is He saying?"

Jesus is saying that we should learn to be more like Him, we should be more gentle and humble; and after growing in those virtues we can find rest for our souls. This isn't a promise that all our difficulties will just vanish before us, but that we will learn how to better handle those difficulties and experience rest no matter what is going on around us. Christ's yoke is easy, and His burden is light because He has the strength to take on every disappointment without wavering in His faith in the Father.

With this in mind, it's important that we recognize Christ's role as more than Teacher, but also as Helper. He doesn't expect us to be able to do it all on our own. After all, He tells us to come to Him before anything else. This is where it might be helpful to discuss what it means to take Christ's yoke. Christ would have been speaking in Greek, so it sometimes helps to figure out what the words Jesus used would have meant to His original audience. The word "easy" would have meant "useful, manageable, serviceable", and "light" would have meant "light in weight."

Using those definitions, we can get a better understanding of Christ's teaching as an offer for us to submit to Him. We can submit to His strength and put ourselves under His guidance[19]. This is where it all comes together. Christ is literally saying that what we are about to do, when we take on His burden, will be useful for us. He doesn't say it will be "easy" like we use the word "easy", but that it will be something that will be designed to fit our needs. Better still, He promises to be there with us, and that's an amazing offer coming from the Divine. Jesus is not content with watching everything happen, He is willing to join us in our mess and help us get through it.

Even in His promises to make our lives easier, Christ is sure to include the need for us to submit ourselves to Him. It is only through our submission that we can experience true rest. This promise isn't about us, or at least not the way we expect it to be. Jesus is promising to be with us and to make our lives better, yes. But He is only willing to do so if we are willing to lay down our own desires and our own pride and allow Him to lead the way for us. We don't have to worry about figuring out which way to go because He has determined the path already. Christ is presenting us the invitation to simply rest and follow Him, and that's a whole lot easier than trying to do it on our own.

---

19 Keathley, J. Hampton. "The Call To Discipleship: An Invitation To Rest (Matthew 11:28-30)."*Bible.org*, bible.org/article/call-discipleship-invitation-rest-matthew-1128-30.

ROMANS 8:28

"And we know that God causes everything to work together for the good of those who love God and are called according to his purpose for them."

Romans 8:28 may be used as a verse of encouragement in times of trouble, but it does not mean that everything is good. In fact, a reading of this verse from a new believer would likely be met with nothing but confusion. It's hard to understand how God could use something inherently bad like cancer, AIDS, or a broken family for anything good. So, let's see what Romans 8:28 is saying by determining who wrote it to whom, when, where, and why?

CONTEXT

The book of Romans is a letter from the Apostle Paul to the church in Rome. Paul was once the biggest persecutor of Christians but ended up writing almost half the New Testament. This letter is one of many epistles the apostle wrote to churches which he had visited or had some previous contact with during his missionary journeys. In fact, Paul probably wrote Romans during his third missionary journey from Corinth, a little more than 20 years after the Jesus ascended into heaven. [20]

Paul had never visited the group of Christians whom he

---

20 Malick, David. "An Introduction To The Book Of Romans." *Bible.org*, bible.org/article/introduction-book-romans.

was addressing in Romans, but he knew that Rome was the center of the Empire and was an ethnically diverse city. This is important information because it meant that Paul was writing to a community that consisted of individuals from all social classes and backgrounds.[21] He did not confine his teaching to a closed audience, but instructed with an overview meant to apply to many contexts.

Since he had never visited the church in Rome, Paul didn't spend much time writing on specific issues that were going on within the church because he simply didn't know what the key issues were. Instead, Paul wrote a short version of the whole Gospel covering everything from creation, sin, and redemption, all the way to eventual restoration.[22] Paul wrote this letter to address some issues occurring within the church of Rome, to introduce himself to his readers, and to systematically defend his teaching by providing an overview of his Gospel.

CONNECTION

If we look at the verses leading up to verse 28, Paul is talking about the present sufferings that Christians must go through while we wait "for that future day when God will reveal who his children really are" (8:19). Paul opens with an admittance that not everything that happens is good, otherwise why would

---

21 "Introduction to the Epistle to the Romans." *Blue Letter Bible*, www.blueletterbible.org/study/intros/romans.cfm.

22 Lawrenz, Mel. "Who Was Paul, and How Should We Understand His Epistles?" *Bible Gateway Blog*, 22 June 2016, www.biblegateway.com/blog/2015/04/who-was-paul-and-how-should-we-understand-his-epistles/.

he admit to any suffering.

Instead, Paul is saying that this suffering does not compare to the joy we will have in eternity. He is not denying suffering but providing a sense of freedom despite that suffering. He goes on to encourage the Romans to have hope even when they can't see what they are hoping for. The Spirit, Paul says, will be there to help Christians in times of weakness and will talk to God for us with words that we could not express.

Like the prophet Jeremiah, Paul isn't giving the Romans an easy fix by saying everything will be okay. No, he is reminding this young church that they are part of something much bigger than themselves. Not everything that happens will be good, I'm sure we can all agree with that, but the Spirit's work in us is a promise that all things are working together towards the ultimate good.

In this case, it might help to view 'good' as a thing to be achieved and not just a description of the current state of affairs. Anyone who has spent years of practice to perfect a certain talent knows what Paul is talking about here. Not every day of practice was good. Maybe you sprained an ankle, broke a string, had something fall apart, or just had a bad day. Those things were not good, but if you were able to keep working through the hard days, chances are you got to a point where the fruit of your labor was evident, and your skills were significantly more advanced than you would have been if you hadn't experienced those difficulties and setbacks.

Christianity is kind of like practicing a skill; but it is part of a story that is indescribably complex. Despite the differences between Christianity and a usual talent, we can still compare the two and realize that what Paul is saying is that, despite the times of difficulty which we will experience, we can be sure that God is working for The Good of all who believe in Him.

HEBREWS 13:5

"Don't love money; be satisfied with what you have. For God has said,
"I will never fail you.
I will never abandon you."

Hebrews 13:5 addresses one of the most common topics in the Bible: money. Church services often revolve around church finances, young adults are told not to make money an idol, and church boards spend many nights discussing budgets and funds. In all these situations, Christians find themselves coming back to verses like Hebrews 13:5 to calm their fears and remember to be content with what they have.

This desire for contentment is, in many cases, exactly what is needed in that situation. Considering its relevance, let's see what the context was when this verse was written, and give the Scripture a chance to express more than the surface-level meaning and speak even deeper into our lives.

CONTEXT

The author of the book of Hebrews is not known. Despite many attempts to dissect the book and determine the most likely author, there is no way of knowing for sure who was writing or who they were writing to. Most likely, the author was a former Jew writing to other former Jews. We can make that assumption because the book warns the readers against the dangers of going back to Judaism, and supports the superiority of Christ.[23] Since we cannot know for sure who is involved in Hebrews, it's hard to determine what is going on that made the author want to write. That, too, is hard to determine because the book is kind of written like a letter, but it reads like a cluster of sermons strung together.

While we may not be clear about the history of Hebrews, we can determine that the book is written to encourage and instruct believers in Christ, so it can't be completely off-base to say that this book is simply an overview of the Christian faith, written to address issues faced by all Christians.

CONNECTION

If Hebrews is a synopsis of issues faced by all Christians, then it's important that we investigate the full depth of the topics discussed. Leading into chapter 13, the author talks about the Son's superiority over all things, specifically focusing on angels. This discourse is followed by warnings about what we will go through as humans, and against falling away from the faith.

So, this is a book written to encourage Christians and warn them against falling away from the most powerful being, Jesus Christ. Chapter 13 is the concluding chapter of the book and serves as a summary of the important parts of being a Christian. This is the part where the author gives his readers some practical advice after numerous theological reflections.

To put it simply, the author says to love each other, be kind to all people, visit those in prison, that marriage is good if it

---

23 Malick, David. "An Introduction To The Book Of Hebrews." *Bible.org*, 17 Jan. 2014, bible.org/article/introduction-book-hebrews.

is pure, and, then, to keep free from the love of money. But this advice is much bigger than it seems, because the author includes God's promise to never leave or forsake anyone as part of the advice to be wary of greed. This isn't just a trite comment, it's an assurance that God has promised to take care of all our needs, even financially.

When we can eliminate our love for money, then we have more time to focus on loving God, and God promises to take care of the rest. In fact, we should do more than just not love money, we should be happy with what we already have.

If you're looking for a catchphrase, you could simplify this to say that Christians should live with an 'attitude of gratitude'. We shouldn't be focused on always getting more, but we should be happy with what God has already given us, and remember to be thankful that He has promised to continue to provide for our necessities.

God's promise will hold true in all situations, and Hebrews 13:5 re-presents an Old Testament promise from God that He is willing and able to provide everything we need for a happy, healthy life. If we can fix our eyes on Christ instead of money, then we are able to take part in an eternal promise of God's community.

It's Not About You

So far, we have seen a few examples of how reading one Bible verse can result in different understandings depending on how you read it. These are meant to show that the popular opinion is not always the best one, and it certainly isn't the only one. The verses that we have looked at are meant to show a process of contextual interpretation that can aid us in our desire to know God better. While this is certainly not the only way to read the Bible, and you may find it isn't the best way for you, it is an important aspect of the Christian lifestyle to continually build a deeper relationship with God and in-depth, contextual scriptural study is a great way of doing just that. It is important to our faith that we seek to appreciate the significance of each verse and how it relates to the truth of God's Kingdom.

Contextual interpretation says that in order to explain a verse's contemporary meaning, we have to first figure out what it would have meant when it was written down. We wouldn't take a verse like 1 Samuel 1:10, "Hannah was in deep anguish, crying bitterly as she prayed to the Lord", and assume that we could know what was going on without at least looking at the rest of the chapter, so why would we try to do so with any other verse? The chapters and books surrounding the verse are the first clues showing us what else is going on that could affect the verse's meaning. We have to get to know the Bible in order to understand it.

GETTING TO KNOW THE BIBLE

The Bible is more of a conversation than many of us often realize. Its nature makes it important for us to not only take in what it is saying, but also to respond to it and engage with it. Any good conversationalist knows that a key to engaging in a meaningful discussion is for both participants to have an idea of where the other is coming from. That means knowing part of their background, beliefs, life experiences, where they're from, their dreams and desires; anything that makes them unique from every other person. Our conversation with the Bible is no different. We need to understand the author, the audience, the physical setting, the historical setting, and anything else that could play a part in shaping the environment in which the verse was written. We need to know these things because it all plays into what the verse is trying to show us. When we make these considerations, it is a little bit easier to determine what the verse is trying to tell us. While the words on the page may not change, a more in-depth study into the background of the Bible may give us a completely different understanding of the passage.

It's important to note, here, that this is something that can be done by anyone. Too often in our culture we find ourselves feeling like we either are not qualified, or are not expected to study the Bible, so, why should we? To respond to the first concern, everyone is qualified to study the Bible. Later on, in this chapter, we will talk about the Reformation and what that meant for the common Christian, but for now, suffice it to say that every person is qualified to study the Bible. While some of us have more specific training, the process of interpretation which we are talking about is nothing more than engaging with a specific verse by considering what else is going on in the chapter, book, and the whole Bible. This is something that can be done no matter what level of Biblical scholarship you have attained. It follows, then, that the second concern is just something we tell ourselves because we are okay with letting someone else do the hard work that comes with studying Scripture. That is also false. If we are God-seeking, image-bearing, children of God, then it is our responsibility to study His word in order to be more like Him. We can never discount the work of the Spirit in our lives, but the best way we can try to be more like God is by engaging with the Word, and that means that God does expect us to study the Bible. In fact, in Matthew 4, Jesus cites an Old Testament verse in responding to temptation by saying, "The Scriptures say, 'People do not live by bread alone, but by every word that comes from the mouth of God" (Matt. 4:4). Jesus realized the life-giving power of the word of God, and that's a good enough argument for me.

So, let's return to how we can get to know the Bible. Part of that process is realizing that we, the other half of the conversation, are continually changing. Each day we have experiences that alter who we are. You are a slightly different person now than you were three words ago. There are changes taking place physically as well as mentally that you cannot control, they just happen. These changes may be so subtle that we hardly notice them, or they can be so obvious that we never forget how it affected who we are and who we want to be. Either way, we complete each day as a slightly different person than we began.

"What does that have with studying the Bible?"

Well, quite a bit. When we come to Scripture, we are bringing our own experiences into that conversation. Each time we read a verse, we are a different person than we were the last time we read that same verse. Now, this doesn't mean that every time we read Jeremiah 29:11 we are going to come to a different understanding of its meaning. Our understanding might not change at all or, if it does, only slightly. But, there is still a chance that our interpretation might be completely different, and we could have a brand-new enlightenment that was impossible for us to have experienced before. This is made possible because of the change that is taking place in our lives. This makes it very important that we don't simply assume we know what a verse means because we heard a sermon on it three years ago. The change that is happening in our lives is one way that God works in us, and so when we come to Scripture with an open mind to new interpretation we are allowing God's work to show itself in the way we understand His Word.

Sometimes, we think we know what a verse means because it seems like everyone else knows what it means too. But, if we are allowing change to work in our lives, then we should realize that a verse's popularity does not make it immune from greater study. We may think we know everything we need to know about a verse or passage simply because we have heard it repeated so many times, but one of the fascinating things about studying the Bible is its ability to reveal new meanings every time you pick it up. That's what makes Christianity a relationship that is forever changing and growing. One way to aid our spiritual growth is by recognizing the need to continually reevaluate Scripture. When we realize that we are changing, we can come to Scripture ready to have a meaningful conversation born out of the work God is doing in us.

The title of this chapter is meant to arouse some curiosity, and it probably seems a little odd that we've spent the first portion of this section talking about the individual and how we should come to the Bible when the title is pointing away from the individual. But the point we should get from this first section is that the Bible is not necessarily trying to answer every question you ask of it. We talked about how we are changing and how that affects our conversation with the Bible, but we also should realize that we are never going to be intelligent enough to understand every verse on our own. The work of the Holy Spirit is to show us what we need to know at each point in our lives. That means that, sometimes, we simply are not meant to know the answer to our question. If God answered every question we have of Him, there would be little use for the work of faith in our lives. Sometimes, it is in the best interest for our relationship with God to simply understand His love for us, without necessarily getting an answer to our questions. With that in mind, we should also realize that leaving a conversation with Scripture feeling like nothing has changed is not always a bad thing, sometimes that means we were looking for the wrong thing. When we come to Scripture looking for answers, we are forgetting that the Bible is about God. It is one of God's ways of conversing with Creation, but it is not a guidebook of FAQ's. It is a description of the Kingdom and the characteristics of God through human language.

There are times when reading the Bible with a specific question in mind is valuable and helpful. However, we should not come to the Bible with a specific question to be answered every time we open the cover. Why? Well, now we get to the title of the chapter. Because the Bible is not about you. If we think that the Bible exists to answer our personal needs, that's just wrong.

WHO IS IT ABOUT?

The Bible wasn't written with any one individual in mind. Rather, the Bible was written for every person that is living or has ever lived. That's a lot of eyes looking at the same words. Even if we narrow it down to the people who are attending Christian churches on a given Sunday, we are talking about billions of people who get together every week for the same purpose: to encounter the Divine in community. If we expand that across history, that means that every aspect of Christianity, and especially Scripture, is relevant to an innumerable audience. Christianity is not about you, and it's not about me, and it's not about any one human person. It wasn't written with one individual in mind, because it was written with every individual in mind. It was written to describe God and His Kingdom, and it is equally important for every person.

The Early Church understood this, and it showed in their daily lives. They met nearly every day, not just once a week, and not just with a smile and nod across the sanctuary. In fact, they often chose to meet in the intimacy of their own homes. They continued to meet in the synagogues and temples, as most early Christians were converted Jews, but their commitment to meeting in homes also shows their deep commitment and familiarity with one another. Much of this can be seen in Acts chapter 2, but, why does this matter to us?

It matters because they realized that being a Christian means being part of a group, a collective, a Community with one goal in mind; to get to know God and to serve Him. They realized the simplicity of Christianity is to grow together, not to become isolated individuals bent over their Bibles and scribbling their thoughts in a notebook all day. A lone-wolf mindset will not get you very far.

You say, "where's your proof?" I say, "read the Bible!"

Jesus tells us repeatedly to love each other and teaches us in John 17 about the importance of coming together. Paul probably had carpal tunnel from writing about church unity so much, and that's just scratching the surface. David got the idea in Psalm 133: "How wonderful and pleasant it is when brothers live together in harmony!" Peter talked about Christians as "living stones that God is building into his spiritual temple" and goes on to call Christians a "chosen people. You are royal priests, a holy nation, God's very own possession" (1 Peter 2). In more than one letter, Paul speaks of the individual as a member of Christ's body, and calls us all sons of God. The Old Testament is all about instituting the nation of Israel as God's people, and the Early Church understood that Christ made the distinction of 'God's people' available to all who seek Him. This is not to say that the Early Church was perfect – far from it. The Church has always had its issues no matter what historical period we are talking about, but the Early Church did seem to understand that they were all in it together. While that feeling probably didn't lead to well-choreographed musical numbers (High School Musical, anyone?), it did help create an obvious feeling of intimacy in their relationships. One possible cause for this intimacy is the persecution these first Christians were enduring because of their new faith. These renegade believers probably felt like it was them against the rest of the world, which would have certainly created an intense feeling of reliance on one another. The interesting thing is, while persecution may have been the cause of the Church's intimacy, can we also consider that it could have been the effect? Could the Church members' obvious love for one another have stirred up some feelings of jealousy or resentment that only spurred on their persecutors? Maybe, maybe not. But it is fascinating to think about the effect this environment of love might have had on the ancient world if there were more persecutors that had an experience like Saul of Tarsus (Acts 9).

While we can't say that today's Western church experiences widespread persecution like that of the early believers, we should never use that as an excuse to forget about the believers across the world who are experiencing very real persecution in our own time. It's easy to forget that Christianity has such a global reach when we go to the same church, hear the same pastor, and see the same people once a week, but that's not what Christianity is about. There's a great big world outside of our comfortable bubbles, and we simply must realize that the Church is made up of more people than we could ever know.

Once we start to grasp the scope of Christianity, it is even more interesting to consider how one religion can take so many different forms. What started with a carpenter and his friends now requires an entire lexicon of characteristics used just to describe the differences between Christ-followers. Even if we skip the initial divisions between Christians, the last time the Church was even moderately united was the early 1500's (and that's if we overlook the Great Schism of 1054), when we followed the doctrines put in place by the Roman Catholic Church. Then came Lutherans, Anabaptists, Calvinists, Anglicans, Baptists, Quakers, Pietism, and Wesleyans, and that only gets us to the 1800's. Next came the Brethren, Mormons, Seventh-Day Adventists, Jehovah's Witnesses, and Pentecostals. But wait, there's more. The twentieth and twenty-first centuries have brought on more 'movements' and termed them Evangelicalism, Ecumenism, and Fundamentalism, to name a few[24]. The crazy thing is, we haven't even scratched the surface. We have said nothing of the distinction between the Eastern and Western Church; let alone those further divisions we call denominations. If you consider just the 'splits', we still have Catholics, Protestants, and Orthodox bases for faith. So, the obvious question is, how did we get here? While we could spend forever discussing church history, it's probably easiest to start with that first big split, when a German monk unknowingly set the Christian world on a path which has forever shaped its history.

---

24 http://www.astudyofdenominations.com/overview/

RELEVANCE OF THE REFORMATION

When Martin Luther kickstarted the Protestant Reformation, he set into motion something much bigger than he ever had in mind. His attempt to reform the Catholic Church resulted in a complete restructuring of Christianity that eventually led to the diverse denominational landscape that we have today. Without making this too much of a history lesson, what we should recognize is that one of the greatest things Luther accomplished was making Scripture accessible to the average person, and it's important that we consider the affect that had on the Community of God.

Before the Reformation, scriptural study was reserved for church leaders only. The Bible was not mass-produced, and you could not find it in every Christian household as you can today. In fact, even if it were mass-produced, the average person would not have been able to read it because it had not yet been translated out of Latin into the languages spoken by the masses. This meant that the clergy had complete control over the spiritual lives of their followers. The clergy saw their opportunity and they capitalized. To summarize, the priests of the time led their congregations to believe that they could buy their salvation so that they could put a little more money into their own robes, and no one could call the priests on their dishonesty because no one besides the priests could study the Bible. See the problem? Luther did. In one of his writings describing the grievances of the German people, he described this misdeed, saying, "Although spiritual penance ought to be imposed upon sinners for one reason only, namely to gain salvation of their souls, ecclesiastical judges tend to penalize so formidably that sinners are obliged to buy their way out. This practice caused enormous amounts of money to flow into the church's treasury". [25]

Luther's attempts to reform the Church came in many writings. Some of which were extremely formative in the development of beliefs that are now commonplace in Protestant Christianity. Rather than delving into each of these radical, transformative beliefs, we will consider Luther's realization that salvation is a matter affecting God and an individual. He understood that the relationship was one in which God valued the individual, as well as the greater whole.[26]

It was in 1520 that Luther's reformative theology really got the world turning. The invention of the printing press created an opportunity for Luther to appeal directly to the masses without engaging the clerics and academics of the time. He wrote in a language that could be understood by the German people, and in doing so, included those who were traditionally marginalized by the religious elite. He published three works in 1520; *The Appeal to the Nobility of the German Nation*, *The Babylonian Captivity of the Church*, and *The Freedom of a Christian*.

In his *Appeal to the Nobility of the German Nation*, Luther outlined his critique against the Church by saying that it had shielded itself from criticism by drawing a distinction between laity

---

25 Hillerbrand, Hans J., and Martin Luther. "The Grievances of the German People." *The Protestant Reformation*, Harper Perennial, 2009, pp. 3–13.

26 McGrath, Alister E. "The Accidental Revolutionary." *Christianity's Dangerous Idea*, HarperOne, 2008, pp. 37–45.

and clergy. In doing so, the Church declared the government of the Church to be a matter reserved to the clergy, which lowered the place of the laity. The Church also flat-out denied the laity the right to interpret the Bible. These defenses kept the Church safe from criticism and, therefore, from any sort of reform. Luther saw the problems this created and declared that it was time for these defenses to come down.

Luther cited the New Testament and outlined one of the greatest themes of the Reformation – the democratization of faith. He referred to the Church as a community of believers rather than a divinely ordained institution with power belonging only to the clergy. He founded his belief in the New Testament's portrayal of the Church as a "priesthood of all believers" and said that there was no scriptural evidence for the superiority of the clergy over the laity. Rather, Luther presented the idea of a "priesthood of all believers", which meant, among other things, that every Christian should have the right to interpret the Bible, and therefore, to critique any of the Church's teachings or practice that may appear to diverge from the teachings of the Bible.

The only authority the clergy had, according to Luther, was given directly by the laity. This authority was merely a result of recognizing individuals within the church who had some special gifts and were therefore given the role of teaching among the congregation. This should not detract from the birthright of believers to have the opportunity to read and understand the Bible in a language they were familiar with. Luther's call for reform, coupled with the invention of the printing press, led to a revolution that would forever change the Christian world. [27]

As the Bible was suddenly available to the masses, it caused something that Luther did not intend. The Catholic Church was unable to cope with this revolutionary call for change, and the schism between Catholic and Protestant had begun. Luther's empowering of all believers gave every person the ability to publicize their own interpretation based on their own understanding of Scripture. As individual community leaders began promoting their own interpretations, the public began to splinter into factions following one leader or the other. My favorite book regarding the Reformation, if you wish to see this more in-depth, is *Christianity's Dangerous Idea*, by Alister McGrath. But what we get if we replay that fracturing over and over for a couple hundred years, is a Protestant landscape consisting of hundreds of denominations that make up a large portion of today's Church.

Today, with the introduction of the internet and smart-phones, we are living in a world with more access to Scripture than any generation in history. We can log onto social media and share our thoughts on any topic in a matter of seconds, and so can a large portion of the world's population. Not only can we share our own thoughts, we are also able to read an innumerable amount of ideas about our Bible. This hyper-scripturalized world is, for many, a dream come true. Like the laypeople of Luther's time, we now have a chance to make our thoughts known to a much wider audience and we

27 McGrath, Alister E. "The Accidental Revolutionary." *Christianity's Dangerous Idea*, HarperOne, 2008, pp. 50-53.

can do so far easier than ever before. However, with such great opportunity comes an even greater responsibility.

OUR RESPONSIBILTY

If we are going to share our thoughts on any verse, and have it made available to such a wide audience, then we need to consider, or at least try to consider, every possible angle of inter-pretation. A post to Facebook may seem harmless, but we need to realize that it reflects more than just our own thoughts. It is also a representation of the importance of the Bible and Chris-tianity and could serve as a rare contact point with someone who is not used to engaging with Scripture on a daily basis. If we are to share our own thoughts, then it is necessary that we know what we are talking about first.

Proper study and interpretation not only aids your own spiritual growth, it can also have a profound impact on the growth and understanding of anyone with whom you share your thoughts. This is a potentially wonderful, but also poten-tially devastating byproduct of life in the Community. Just as we should consider the inner workings of both parties in our conversation with Scripture, we should also seek to understand the context of our personal conversations, meaning that we have to understand that we are greatly affected by our own surroundings and so is every other person.

There is no such thing as an unbiased interpretation of Scripture, because every person who has ever lived has been a product of the context in which they live. To be biased is to be human, and it is not a bad thing. Every moment that you have ever lived in has made a difference in how you come to

Scripture, so it is impossible to not have some sort of preconception that affects your interpretation. Even if you have never encountered Christianity before, you would still have some ideas about morality or the world that would affect how you understand the teachings of the Bible. As we realize this about ourselves, it can help us see how important it is to be careful about sharing our ideas with others, because they are going through the same thing. We should not be scared to share our ideas, in fact sharing ideas is the only way we can truly grow. However, we should certainly read Scripture prayerfully and with constant evaluation, and we should engage in any conversation about Scripture in the same way.

Christianity is many-layered. For any conversation to be effective, both parties need to take each other's context into account. In the same way, we can see that is it necessary to consider the context of Scripture, and to look at the history of Christianity that Scripture is providing. When we read the Bible, we are reading thousands of years of history. It is a history that is focused on the Kingdom, not Creation. That distinction is important. While we could argue that Creation is part of the Kingdom, and in a way it is, we have to realize that Scripture is not focused on providing a biological, ecological, historical account of the earth. It is not a word-for-word portrayal of everything that has ever happened, but it is a multi-generational depiction of the history of Christianity, which is the best point of reference for the story of God's people.

FAITH AND FREEDOM

One of the many shortcomings of life on earth is our inability to completely understand the nature of God. We will never know the Kingdom of God in its fullness until we experience it. Despite all our attempts to make the Kingdom known, we will never know if we got it right until we come into the real thing. So how can we be sure it even exists? Well, it helps that we have proof.

The Bible provides a physical testament of Christianity as an eternal Community. This book is something that God has given us as a foundation for our faith. Thanks to Luther, we believe that faith is all that is necessary for salvation, but for faith to exist it has to have something to be grounded upon, and the Bible provides a big part of that foundation.

When we see the Bible as a historical insight into the Kingdom, we can start to recognize that what all people see as a desire to discern the 'Meaning of Life' could be nothing more than a subconscious craving to experience the Community of God, or at least something like it. Our desire is to be part of something that is bigger than ourselves. Call it the Holy Spirit or human nature, but when we look at the society's tendency towards restlessness – always looking for a reason to start a revolution or institute a new set of ideals – it seems to me that those experiences are examples of individuals trying to come to terms with the fact that they are not as big of a deal as they once thought. Our time will end; and when we realize that fact, our natural inclination is to seek out something of lasting value, and through that larger narrative, allow ourselves to feel as if we have more meaning.

The great news is that the Bible, when studied in context, presents that 'something bigger' that every person is seeking. The Father of the Kingdom desperately wants all His children to spend eternity with Him. The Community of God is a Kingdom that envelopes all of us into a never-ending narrative of love and victory. Our desire to conquer death is made possible by Christ's gift of redemption and fellowship with the Father. The answers we are looking for are right in front of us, and God is eagerly presenting those answers so that we can join Him.

Ultimately, it's not about you, me, or any of our individual achievements. All these things will eventually be forgotten and will do nothing to boost our resumes in the Kingdom. We may look at certain titans of the Christian faith and think that their influence will never cease. But more often than not, the reason we even know their names is because they realized their role in history was not to advance their own reputation but to point their audiences to the One whose time will never end. The greatest thing any of us can do is to accept that our position as part of the Community makes us servants to our Creator. When we do so, our desire to be part of something bigger is fulfilled and we will be compelled to send the invitation to the Kingdom even further so that all may experience the freedom found in Community.

It's not about us because the Bible is more than just a 'love letter' from God to us. While it is a piece of literature that describes God's continual provisions of love and grace to Creation, the idea that these words are meant for nothing more than for God to prove His love to us is, frankly, kind of selfish. If we minimize the impact of the Word to a mere proof of God's love for us, we are disregarding the overarching narrative of God's eternal power. God is love. But God is also truth, hope, grace, light, compassion, justice, and power. The Bible is about the love of God, and that may even be the main point, but it is not the only point. There is much more to the Bible than love, and there is much more to the Bible than us.

The Bible is not about any one person, it is about God and His Kingdom.

While the stories of Abraham, Isaac, Jacob, David, John the Baptist, the Disciples, and every other individual except for One find an ending in Scripture, the ceaseless narrative of God's nature extends beyond the covers of the book and engulfs eternity. More than that, it is eternity. The Kingdom of God is the reason the Book exists. The characters depicted on its pages have been venerated to near-heroic status in the Christian tradition, but in truth, these men and women are no more heroic than any other human in the history of humankind. Jesus saw the temptation to worship God's people in place of God and told the Jews of His day:

> *"You search the Scriptures because you think they give you eternal life. But the Scriptures point to me! Yet you refuse to come to me to receive this life…If you really believed Moses, you would believe me, because he wrote about me."*
> *John 5:39-40, 46*

Like anyone else, our time will end. But if we can realize what Moses, Jeremiah, James, Mary Magdalene, and Peter all realized – that we are but pieces of the grand puzzle that is the Community of God – then we should eagerly accept our responsibility as image-bearers of the Father.

This is exciting!

Nothing should be able to hold back our joy at being invited into the Kingdom of God.

We may never write the next book of the Bible, but that does not diminish our role in the slightest. Our lives are just as important because each one of us is making an impact every day in the lives of those around us. Some of the most influential participants in the Community of God will never have a book written about them, directly because they were able to fulfill Christ's call on their lives by placing a higher priority on Community empowerment than their own ambitions.

Near the end of Matthew 16, Jesus presents the point I am trying to make by telling His disciples, "If any of you wants to be my follower, you must give up your own way, take up your cross, and follow me" (Matt. 16:24). Jesus is saying that our lives are not even about us, for we can only find our lives by losing them for Jesus's sake. He continues by saying, "What do you benefit if you gain the whole world but lose your own soul? Is anything worth more than your soul?" Here, Jesus is alluding to the eternal relevance that can only come by way of a commitment to the Kingdom. He affirms this by saying, "For the Son of Man will come with his angels in the glory of his Father and will judge all people according to their deeds. And I tell you the truth, some standing here right now will not die before they see the Son of Man coming in his Kingdom."

By denying ourselves, we are admitting our mortality and

submitting ourselves to a life of eternity with God. It may seem backward at first because we are rejecting our natural tendencies to put ourselves first. Yet, if we are to have any life at all, then we have to combat our human nature with an immense faith that accomplishes what our true nature desires most. We are taking part in a marvelous 'something bigger', a Kingdom that has no end.

When it comes down to it, our lives are not about ourselves, and Jesus is letting us know. We can whittle that point down to these few verses and move on with our lives, or we can consider the verses we have already studied alongside the many more verses in the Bible that prove the same idea – that this life is not about you. Solomon said, "For everything there is a season, a time for every activity under heaven" (Ecclesiastes 3) but notice the implication that there is not a time for matters that take place in heaven. There is no time for the cessation of the Kingdom.

We should allow the eternal nature of the Kingdom to be our fuel for its expansion. It is only by sharing our beliefs that we can have any hope of making the world aware of the invitation to Community that is available to everyone. Christ's call for us to deny ourselves comes with a command that we go. Placing God's priorities as our own means we can no longer hide our beliefs, but that we take them wherever we go, and it is even more necessary that we go wherever Christ calls us. It shouldn't take a whale to swallow us and spit us out for us to go where we are needed, but if that's what it takes then we have proof in Scripture that God will do whatever it takes to get us where He needs us to be. As we recognize that all of humanity is welcome in the Kingdom, we cannot be selfish and refuse to extend the invitation. It becomes our responsibility to go to every nation and invite every person to join us where they belong.

This Community of God is made up of individuals just like you and I, and for the Community to be made more tangible, welcoming, and present in the lives of individuals around the world, we need to act our part with a sense of love as well as responsibility. In the Bible, God is presenting an opportunity to be part of the only Community that extends throughout eternity. We cannot take that opportunity lightly, and we cannot forget to seek to better understand the majesty of the God we worship. It's not about you; it's about us. The Bible, Christianity, and all of life is about the expansion and continuation of the Kingdom of God; but for that to happen, there must be individuals that are willing to deny our own ambitions and go with Christ.

It's About Us

We have seen that the Bible is an invitation, and that our ambitions should cease to be self-centered and instead should focus on the good of the Kingdom. We should be getting a grasp of the idea that God's intention is for us to live in Community, and that the Bible is a book about Christ – not about us. Our focus should be broadening in order to include a vast number of souls rather than just our own. Now it's time to see how this should impact our lives, and how we can be daily participants in the Community of God.

SELF-REFLECTION

In order to take part in the Community of God, it's important that we understand ourselves as much as we can. This isn't something that we can accomplish in a singular moment, in fact it is just the opposite. Getting to know ourselves is a lifelong journey. For some of us, that journey is filled with joy and delight; for others, it will mean some difficult realizations and even more difficult growing pains. It's enough work to simply survive in a world plagued by sin and darkness, how can anyone have time to devote to personal growth and self-reflection?

Self-reflection will almost certainly be difficult at some points, but continual evaluation is vital for anyone determined to play a role in the Kingdom of God. We can draw a parallel between our need for self-improvement and the history of the Church at the time of the Protestant Reformation.

Remember, when Martin Luther set the Reformation into motion, his goal wasn't the complete upheaval of the Catholic Church. Rather, he was attempting to analyze the Church's shortcomings in order to improve Catholicism so that it would more closely support some key Biblical principles. The essence of Protestantism and the protest which it is promoting is not division but revision. It is a formative act meant to repair that which is broken rather than throwing everything away and starting anew.

As history tells us, and as we have already discussed, Luther's idea of fixing what was broken in the Church wasn't entirely successful. For the Church, Protestantism introduced the key act of healthy criticism by refusing to settle for what has been accepted as ultimate knowledge in favor of a continual renewing of Christian culture. Protestantism is saying that we shouldn't throw away the body simply because one finger is broken, but that we should take the time to fix the finger for the betterment of the entire body. In this situation, the body is more important than its individual parts. It takes careful attention to ensure that each part is performing to its full capability, but all the while the motive is the overall health of the Body.

The same should be true of our personal protest. Even if it sometimes feels like our entire belief system needs to be reinvented, our goal should be to fix what is broken and leave the rest as it was. The goal is not self-destruction but self-rejuvenation and the best way to accomplish this task is by repeatedly examining ourselves.

As individuals, we need to exist in a state of continual renewal and evaluation. We should never come to a place where we feel that we cannot improve in our walk with God, but should always look for what could be improved or, at the very least, reevaluated for our lives to be more firmly grounded in Christ. We don't have to rebuild our entire faith, but we can and should seek to continually protest our own beliefs so that we avoid falling into any sort of complacency. As we do so, we can discover those ideas that are vital to our faith, and those things that we can admit we are uncertain about. Rather than struggling to find the right answer to everything, it is sometimes healthier to admit our inability to comprehend the inconceivable totality of the Divine.

For us to be of any use to the Body, we need to make sure we are taking care of ourselves. As parts of the whole, it is our responsibility to perform to the best of our abilities. Sometimes that means calling out to other members for assistance when we are hurting, but we should always keep in mind the health of the Body as we are healing ourselves. The reality is that our lives affect all of Christianity in some manner, so we should keep track of our own health to improve and maintain the health of the Community.

Self-identification means more than recognizing that we are one among many. It also means we have the freedom to identify our own strengths and weaknesses and respond accordingly. In

1 Peter 4, Peter speaks to a vast audience of believers on the topic of living for God. Among many key points, he communicates to his readers that "God has given each of you a gift from his great variety of spiritual gifts. Use them well to serve one another." The use of the phrase 'he has received' implies that the talents we have are not of our own accord but are truly gifts from God. This also leads into the implication that when we use our talents we are merely giving back to God what was His to begin with. We would be remiss to receive a gift from our Father and not use it for its intended purpose. Doing so would be hurtful to our Father and an act of ingratitude on our part. If we wish to show our thankfulness to God, it's the least we can do to use what talents He has bestowed upon us for the good of administering God's grace to others.

Identifying our own weaknesses provides an opportunity for us to allow Christ to work in us to make us strong. Paul sets an example in 2 Corinthians 12 of how we should treat our weaknesses, saying that we should boast in them because we are recognizing Christ's ability to make His power perfect in our weakness. When we can no longer rely on our own strength and we are forced to turn to Christ instead, we are able to realize the power that has been available to us in Christ all along. It is only in those moments that we are capable of our fullest potential because we must rely on God to work in us.

It is vital that in moments of strength and of weakness that we allow our emotions to have some impact on our thoughts. This doesn't mean allowing our emotions to take over and make decisions for us, but it does mean we need to be aware of how we are feeling and how that is affecting our thoughts. It is not a bad thing to be emotional. Christ experienced intense anguish as well as moments of joy. However, it is important to realize that some things, such as anger or grief, are simply not worth the time and energy they take out of us. While you could argue that both, and certainly grief, are important to emotional health, part of understanding our emotions means recognizing when we should move on. In times of great loss, grief is necessary for the soul to recuperate, but when our time of grief becomes one of dwelling it is better to seek renewal rather than staying in the same state of emotional turmoil. Regardless of the situation, it is important that we are aware of our feelings so that we can live to be more like Christ.

EVIDENCE OF FAITH

Faithfulness is something that encompasses not only belief and feeling, but perhaps more importantly evokes actions that stem from that faith. "God saved you by his grace when you believed..." (Eph. 2:8), this is true, and this is what points us to Christ. At the same time, our faith must result in action. For, "So you see, faith by itself isn't enough. Unless it produces good deeds, it is dead and useless." (James 2:17). To be a Christian is to admit faith in God, and faith in God must result in action. In a book that is focused on the best course of action regarding Scripture, it would be remiss not to discuss how else we may act out our faith.

PRAYER

The act of prayer is much like reading Scripture. It is an act of faithfulness in humility by admitting that God needs to be included in the conversation you have with yourself. You are humbling yourself in that you are conceding total control over your life and recognizing God's ability to speak to and help you in any and every situation. God knows your thoughts and feelings already, but prayer is our way of acknowledging God's sovereignty over our lives.

Jesus gives us an example of how to pray with the Lord's Prayer:

> *"Pray like this:*
> *Our Father in heaven,*
> *may your name be kept holy.*
> *May your Kingdom come soon.*
> *May your will be done on earth,*
> *as it is in heaven.*
> *Give us today the food we need,*
> *and forgive us our sins,*
> *as we have forgiven those who sin against us.*
> *And don't let us yield to temptation,*
> *but rescue us from the evil one."*
> *Matthew 6:9-13*

It is important to note the variance in topics in Jesus' prayer. He begins with a recognition of God's identity as 'our' Father. Here Christ is including Himself with humanity, which further indicates both His humanity and our status as co-heirs with Christ. He identifies God as being 'in heaven' and exemplifies His name as 'hallowed' or 'holy'. He asks that God's kingdom will be made tangible before asking for anything for himself.

Only after making these concessions and requests does Christ ask for anything personal. And even then, the requests Jesus makes are of sustenance—daily bread, forgiveness of sins, and freedom from temptation. These are likely far different requests than those we typically make in prayer.

This doesn't mean that this is all we can pray about, but simply that it is a good starting point. Our prayers can and should extend to every aspect of our lives. Withholding any thoughts from God is not only useless, as God already knows, it is also prideful. Doing so would be telling God, "I want to talk to you about everything except this. This I'm keeping for myself." That's not the type of relationship we are meant to have with the Father. We should be in constant contact throughout our day, continually seeking God's guidance on any matter.

It is in moments of doubt when this act of faithfulness is really tested. For to neglect prayer is to neglect our personal relationship with our Creator. Even if we do not believe the words we are saying, the act of speaking to God is an act of faith because it is recognizing the existence of God, or at least the possibility of existence. We are called to have faith, and even if that faith is only the size of a mustard seed, it is still enough faith to move mountains. Even if our faith is only enough to convince us to move our lips and voice our concerns, it is enough.

The act of memorizing and repeating prayer is another act of faith. It may seem ingenuine to some, as it is easy to forget the meaning of the words you are saying and fall into a pattern of empty choruses, but it is an act of faith nonetheless.

The time and energy spent memorizing a sequence of words meant to be used to interact with the Father is an act of faith because it recognizes the need for interaction. It is dangerous to get to a point where it is empty repetition, but even then, memorized prayer is an act of small faith that can be sufficient.

SACRAMENTS

With the rise of Protestantism came the need for distinguishing what acts should be considered sacramental; that is, an act regarded as an outward and visible sign of an inward and spiritual divine grace. The Catholic Church had always held that there are seven sacraments: the rites of baptism, confirmation, the Eucharist, penance, anointing of the sick, ordination, and matrimony. Martin Luther argued that the number of sacraments should be reduced from seven to two – leaving only the Eucharist and baptism as essential for the Christian faith. This is not to say that the practices of penance, confirmation, anointing, ordination, and matrimony are not worthwhile, just that they are either not symbolic of any spiritual act, or that Christ does not command them.

The beliefs of men like Martin Luther, Ulrich Zwingli, and John Calvin took hold and began dividing the Church into the denominations we see today. Each man differed in their interpretation of the sacraments, yet all three asserted that the sacraments are essential to the Christian life and should be observed regularly in a community of believers.

It's difficult to begin a conversation on the sacraments without delving into the specific differences in the interpretation of their importance and function. Suffice it to say that the act of baptism is a physical act of the inward change God has made in you. Christ's baptism is evidence of the Father's presence in the act and shows the importance of participating in the sacraments as outward testimonies to the Community. Partaking of Christ's body and blood in the Eucharist is another communal act that is a testimony to the remembrance of Christ's sacrifice. Both are actions that represent the importance of unity in community for all believers.

LIFESTYLE OF FAITH

Scripture, prayer, and the sacraments are perfectly good examples of actions that should be taken by Christians. Further, it is vital that we realize that Christianity is not based on actions that can be made by going through the motions, but on a real change in our lifestyle. We can have different interpretations of Scripture, different opinions on the sacraments, and a different experience in prayer, but the result should always be a heart of love for one another.

Prayer is a largely individual practice and does not often engage the larger community. Communal prayer is important, but it doesn't always include the sense of intimacy that we get in private prayer. While the Bible's teaching to pray in secret isn't to discount communal prayer, it does warn against the temptation to flaunt our spiritual prowess in public, which is something that can't happen when we pray in private. The sacraments are outward, communal acts, but they are not enough. These are all things that we do as Christians to engage with the Father in some way, but they are not the end results of a changed heart. A lifestyle of love is the only logical result of faith in God, and a relationship with Him simply must result in love.

When you consider doctrines and biblical interpretation, the question we should be asking ourselves is: What if I'm wrong? Is my faith going to be destroyed if I come to find out that not everything I believe about God and Christianity was correct? Faith is most genuine when it accepts that human knowledge can never be complete. Our attempts at understanding the infinite will never be completely accurate. It's necessary then, that we start to distinguish between those beliefs that are necessary for our faith and those things that are not as essential.

We know that the Bible is several things. 2 Timothy 3:16 says it is "inspired by God and is useful to teach us what is true and make us realize what is wrong in our lives.", Hebrews 4:12 says it is "alive and powerful. It is sharper than the sharpest two-edged sword, cutting between soul and spirit, between joint and marrow. It exposes our innermost thoughts and desires." Scripture is "perfect, reviving, trustworthy, right, radiant, more precious than gold, and sweeter than honey" (Psalm 19). But nowhere can we find any evidence that the Bible is immune to misinterpretation. Any venture into scriptural interpretation is a venture into the unknown, and could result in a misunderstanding of Scripture's intent. Studying the Bible can result in a multitude of different understandings and, though that may seem counterproductive, that is the reality that the Bible must produce, because it is a book of Divine truths that are so true that we cannot always understand them. We misinterpret the Bible because we often misinterpret its intent. It is not a science textbook, and it will not reveal to us the way the earth was created. It is not a word-for-word recounting of the past nor is it a discussion of the physiology of human beings. It is a book of truth that is meant to point us to Christ. The avenues that are available to us create opportunities for different interpretations to coexist and for discussions of opposing viewpoints to come to a common ground in the fact that we don't always know the answer.

FAITH AND SCIENCE

The opportunity for open-mindedness allows things like Christianity and science to coexist and even complement each other. Just because science provides evidence for something that doesn't align with our understanding of the Bible doesn't mean that one of them must be wrong. Maybe it just means that our interpretation of the Bible is wrong. Science can inform our spiritual growth if we allow it. When we admit that science is right about something that seems to contradict Scripture, we aren't saying that the Bible is wrong, but that science is helping us come to a better understanding of what its purpose is. Our faith shouldn't rest on how long it took God to create the earth and everything in it, but on the essential fact that He did create it.

The Church has not been incredibly open to new scientific discoveries historically, just ask guys like Copernicus and Galileo. While the Church did not react violently to their assertions that the earth revolved around the sun, the religious authorities at the time certainly did not welcome this view as they saw it being contradictory to their interpretation of the

Bible. Galileo even ended up on house arrest for a period of time as a result of his publication of his scientific discoveries.

To be clear, Galileo's tale does not mean that the Church is anti-science. Neither does it mean that Christians should accept all scientific assertions without proper discussion. The Bible is not a science textbook, and was never meant to be read as one. But there are some things that the Bible asserts regarding the creation of the universe that should be held firmly. We shouldn't immediately respond to science by saying, "yes, that has to be completely true." But neither should our response be "no, that can't be true." As we reflect on the fallibility of human knowledge and the certainty that no interpretation or set of beliefs is without flaw, our response to science doesn't need to be a resounding "Yes!", but it should welcome the ideas presented by science as possibilities. We need to realize the Bible's intention of pointing us toward Christ and inviting us to take part in His Community and respond to any scientific evidence that does not point us away from Christ as being entirely plausible.

INTERPRETING FAITH

The Bible is vital to the faith, and it is one avenue through which God communicates love and grace to us, but we are running a risk of idolatry if we begin to hold the Bible in higher esteem than the Lord whom it proclaims. Instead, we need to recognize that the Bible's role in Christianity is to point us to Christ and allow Him to reveal Himself to us through the Bible. The Bible is not the beginning nor the end of faith. Faith comes from and ends with God. If we expect the Bible to be the end, we will only find frustration in its complex contradictory nature. We should keep reading and trying to understand the complexity of the infinite, but we should only do so with the humility of realizing that we will never know all the answers.

We are not called to flawless interpretation, but to faith and love in Christ and for one another. Those things that are essential are far fewer than we may think. There's a danger of oversimplification, but one way to tell if we have been faithful to our call is by evaluating our fruits. I don't mean apples and oranges, but those qualities that are attributed those who belong to Jesus Christ. They are called the fruits of the Spirt, and include: "love, joy, peace, patience, kindness, goodness, faithfulness, gentleness, and self-control" (Galatians 5:22). The change that faith has made in our life should be made evident to those around us by these traits residing in our lives.

The Kingdom of God is a kingdom of love and of faith and of acceptance. It rarely makes sense. It is filled with nuances and contradictions and complications of all kinds. But it is always founded on love. In John 18, Jesus is shown praying for his disciples and for all believers on the night He was arrested. Let His prayer reveal His hope for unity in community, and may His words be enough to convince us that this life is truly about us. As Jesus said,

"I am praying not only for these disciples but also for all who will ever believe in me through their message. I pray that they will all be one, just as you and I are one—as you are in me, Father, and I am in you. And may they be in us so that the world will believe you sent me.

I have given them the glory you gave me, so they may be one as we are one. I am in them and you are in me. May they experience such perfect unity that the world will know that you sent me and that you love them as much as you love me. Father, I want these whom you have given me to be with me where I am. Then they can see all the glory you gave me because you loved me even before the world began! O righteous Father, the world doesn't know you, but I do; and these disciples know you sent me. I have revealed you to them, and I will continue to do so. Then your love for me will be in them, and I will be in them."
John 17:20-26

One thing we can be certain of in Scripture and in Christianity is that all things can point us toward Christ. The best lesson we can see from Scripture is the effect that Christ has on the narrative of the Kingdom. The Old Testament is filled with murder, lust, and sin. It presents confusion more than clarity, but only because of the new reality that is presented in the New Testament. When Jesus arrives on the scene, the narrative is no longer one of military conquest, lust, incest, and murder. Instead, while these circumstances unfortunately do not end, Christ presents to us the opportunity to be redeemed from the darkness of the world and live in the peace of His grace.

The Community that was once built on following the laws of the land is now founded on love for one another. We are free from the tendency to look out only for ourselves because we are able to recognize the reality of the eternal Kingdom that Jesus is inviting us to join. The God of the Jews is the God of all people, and we are welcomed into that Community with open arms. The narrative of the Bible, when read with an awareness to context and open to all possible interpretations, is less about dogma and more about devotion. It is an invitation from God that says, "I know you're not perfect. You don't have it all figured out. But neither does anyone else, and that's okay with me. Come, join me and my Kingdom. Find grace, love, and forgiveness with a community in which you can play a significant role." We shouldn't waste time in responding to this invitation. God might have all of eternity to wait but your life is limited. Don't leave God waiting. Respond with your RSVP, don't forget to check +1, and don't be afraid of your host being upset if you bring more than one. The Kingdom is open to all, so I have a feeling God would welcome you all the more if you bring along as many people as you can. This is a party no one wants to miss.

Verses In Context Part III

MATTHEW 6:33

"Seek the Kingdom of God above all else, and live righteously, and he will give you everything you need."

Matthew 6:33 is a verse that can be used to convey many different things, one of the most popular usages being to assure troubled people that all they need to do is focus on God's kingdom first and then they will get whatever else they want. It's easy to take a promise like "he will give you everything you need" and consider it a checklist on your way to personal satisfaction. But is that really what Jesus had in mind when he was talking to his followers in the Sermon on the Mount?

CONTEXT

We find Matthew 6:33 about the middle of one of Jesus' most important sermons, the Sermon on the Mount. As with much of Matthew, we are reading literature that presents Jesus' teachings to new converts in a thematic way. The book is meant to aid evangelism and discipleship, and often uses a similar format to that of the Old Testament by first presenting a promise followed by a fulfillment of that promise. Much of Jesus' teachings follow that formula, and reading Matthew 6:33 it seems pretty clear that is what Jesus is trying to do here.

Leading up to the Sermon on the Mount, Jesus had been gathering a steady following of disciples that followed him wherever he went. To this point in the book of Matthew, Jesus and his band of brothers had travelled through Galilee performing miracles, teaching in synagogues, and preaching the good news of the kingdom. As you can imagine, all these works have started to pique the interest of people all over Syria.

With large crowds coming to Jesus so often, the Son found it necessary to take his closest disciples away from the crowd to teach them some of the specifics of the glory of God's Kingdom. These private tutoring sessions would last until the crowds managed to find them, at which point Jesus would continue His sermon, teaching whoever was present.

The Sermon on the Mount is one of these private meetings that turned into a large teaching opportunity for Jesus. He began the Sermon with what are called The Beatitudes ("blessed are the..."), and continued to teach his audience about the workings of the Kingdom of God. Matthew 6:33 comes during a part of the sermon when Jesus is focused on encouraging his listeners not to worry. Jesus taught that instead of worrying about what you will eat or drink, or about clothes and what you will wear; that God will take care of those things for all his followers because He cares about all His children.

CONNECTION

This is another verse that is incredibly important but can lose some of its impact because of how often it is repeated. We can't take the promise it presents for granted, but neither can we take it to mean something that it doesn't. There are times when a single word can make all the difference, and this is one of those times. Here, it is important to consider the word "these", as in "these things" in verse 33, and tie it back to what Jesus was talking about in the prior verses. In verses 28-32, Jesus tells us not to worry about what you shall eat, drink, or wear, "These things dominate the thoughts of unbelievers, but your heavenly Father already knows all your needs" (v. 32).

You see, Jesus isn't saying that a Kingdom-first mentality will result in everything going your way. All the Son is saying is that God will provide the things necessary for you to live, if you will first seek His Kingdom. The things like food, water, and shelter are what God is promising to provide for His King-dom-seekers. That might not seem quite as glamorous as "all things", but if someone is really seeking the Kingdom first then we can see that food, water, and shelter are the only material things they need to survive. Spiritual sustenance is more than enough for a Kingdom-minded follower.

You may be thinking, "That doesn't seem nearly as exciting as before?"

Sure, God's promise might not seem like that big of a deal at first glance. But that's why we really need to take the time to think about what is going one here. Jesus is saying that the material needs of human beings can be reduced to the basics – food, water, and shelter. All other things are just extra, and the easiest way to realize this is by seeking first the Kingdom.

When we seek the Kingdom, our desires for material satisfaction can never measure up to the wonder we can experience through a relationship with God. Seeking the Kingdom means to follow Jesus' teachings and walk in a right relationship with God. When we can put our minds on things above, we stop worrying about the things on earth that, really, we never had control over anyway.

Does that make a little more sense?

Our daily worries often are only time-wasters that God says we need to forget about and focus on seeking the Kingdom first. Instead of squandering our God-given breath on what the Father has already promised to provide, He allows us the chance to be a part of a much bigger picture; the picture of the eternal Kingdom that is continually creating and growing. That's an astonishing offer that can't be looked over.

A Kingdom mentality is useful for every person to live to their full potential and to have the best relationship with God possible by always searching for ways to grow the Kingdom and have an even deeper relationship with God. Only when we do that can we begin to experience the fullness of God's love for us.

1 CORINTHIANS 10:13

"The temptations in your life are no different from what others experience. And God is faithful. He will not allow the temptation to be more than you can stand. When you are tempted, he will show you a way out so that you can endure."

1 Corinthians 10:13 is an example of a verse that has been whittled down to one catchphrase that is used in many ways, all of which typically forget the context in which the author was writing. When a team is down three games to one in a best-of-seven series, or when someone loses their job, or when anything that seems like a setback happens; this is a verse that is quoted as an attempted encouragement that "God doesn't test us beyond what we can bear." This is basically a slap on the back and a "you-can-do-it" bit of inspiration when it seems like there's nothing else to say. But the apostle Paul might have had something more in mind, and we need to give him a chance to tell us.

CONTEXT

The book of 1 Corinthians is a pastoral letter from Paul addressing some of the problems and divisions that he has heard are happening within the church in Corinth. Paul addresses moral problems, answers questions from the Corinthians, and defends his authority as an apostle of Christ. All his themes focus on the Christian need to surrender one's pride to be a part of the Kingdom of God. [28]

In chapter 10, leading up to verse 13, Paul teaches the Corinthians about some of the mistakes made by the Israelites in the Old Testament. He talks about the need to avoid doing things that might cause a fellow believer to stumble; in this case, he says that even though eating meat sacrificed to an idol is not a sin, if it causes another believer to stumble then it is better to avoid eating meat for the sake of your fellow believer. A similar application could be made to many Christians' stance on alcohol.

Paul goes on to give a couple of other examples of Israel's mistakes. Sexual immorality and testing the Lord are two of those examples. Then, Paul encourages the church to avoid making these same mistakes and to be wary of falling into those same temptations. He is showing the church that, while the circumstances might have been different, the same temptations have been experienced by generations of God-followers and are examples for future generations of what not to do. [29]

CONNECTION

If we just read all of chapter 10 without picking any of the verses apart, we start to see the bigger picture that Paul is trying to paint for the Corinthians. The temptations that the

28 Keathley, Hampton. "I Corinthians: Introduction and Outline." *Bible. org*, 26 June 2004, bible.org/article/i-corinthians-introduction-and-outline.
29 Guzik, David. "Enduring Word Bible Commentary 1 Corinthians Chapter 10." *Enduring Word*, 2013, enduringword.com/bible-commentary/1-corinthians-10/.

Israelites faced, while not the same, are similar enough to the temptations faced by the Corinthians that it shows how important it is to avoid those same temptations.

There are many comparisons that could be made, but they all show that the temptations we are experiencing have been faced by generations of believers. Yet, Paul encourages the Christians that God will not abandon us during any of our earthly struggles. God always provides a way to stand up in the face of temptation.

Now we need to investigate the second part of this verse, about how we are never tempted beyond what we can bear. What exactly does that mean?

Maybe you feel like you've been pushed past your limit before, or maybe you're just not sure if this is good advice for a loved one going through a tough time of temptation. Whatever the case, it's important to realize that Paul is speaking about spiritual temptations. He's not talking about the everyday struggles that we might expect – like losing a game or having a bad day at work – he's talking about temptations like lust, greed, idolatry, pride, etc. These are matters of the soul that hold eternal relevance.

This verse is an encouragement to seek God amid temptation. It's also a challenge to face temptation and conquer it. We might think we can't get through a certain trial, but that's when we need to go through the uncomfortableness that is necessary for growth. The only way to become stronger in Christ is to face things that we never thought we could defeat, and then rely on God to get through them.

When we conquer those situations, we get to experience

God's love more than ever before because we have learned a little more about our need to rely on His strength rather than our own.

That might not sound quite as empowering as a life in which we can handle everything thrown our way, because now we know that we are going to have to face some tough times before we can grow deeper in our relationship with God. But the good news is that when we emerge victorious, we will have a more complete appreciation and understanding of the love God has for us.

JAMES 1:2-3

"Dear brothers and sisters, when troubles of any kind come your way, consider it an opportunity for great joy. For you know that when your faith is tested, your endurance has a chance to grow."

James 1:2 may be one of the most easily confused verses in the Bible. It is used to comfort individuals who are going through any sort of difficult situation as an assurance that any hardship is simply God's way of testing someone's faith so that they draw closer to Him. This is surely a verse that has been debated at many dinner tables as families go through the pains of life and cannot picture how those troubles can lead to joy. So, what exactly did James have in mind when he said to consider negativity a fuel for joy?

CONTEXT

The half-brother of Jesus wrote the self-titled book of James. He's writing less than 20 years after Jesus' ascension to encourage formerly-Jewish believers to live Christian lives, and his book includes lots of practical advice for Christian living.

His readers received these guidelines with fresh eyes since Jesus' influence was still relatively new. This book would have been a handbook of sorts to help them as they began their new faith journey as Christians.[30] It is because of this new faith journey that many of James' readers knew exactly what

---

30 Smith, Jay. *James Summary*, biblehub.com/summary/james/1.htm.

he was talking about when he said, "troubles of any kind." For many of them, that meant unfair treatment by the rest of society who weren't so excited about this group who called themselves 'Christians'.

CONNECTION

Just like this first generation of Christians, believers today experience trials of all kinds. Everyone struggles with something, whether it is a temptation to lie, cheat, or steal; or maybe it's something that we don't have any control over like a death in the family or other emergency.

These situations can make us feel like our lives are getting darker with no hope of the good times returning. When we're in despair, reading a verse like this can seem like nothing more than an apostolic slap in the face and urging to "rub some dirt in it" and keep playing, except James takes it even further by telling Christians not only to keep going but to find joy in our trials.

Before we move on, let's realize that at no point in time did James say this was going to be easy. We would be expecting a lot from ourselves to be put in a tough situation and automatically respond with joy. Although joy is a state of the spirit, whereas happiness is a state of mind, it would still be difficult to train oneself so well as to cling to joy in the face of misery.

Nonetheless, James does say to consider trials joy. So, how do we do it?

The answer lies in verse 3, when James gives us the reason for our joy, "when your faith is tested, your endurance has a chance to grow." Here, James assures his readers that these tests will result in a greater ability to persevere.

The only way to grow is to go through difficulties. To go through difficult situations, a Christian must first build up their perseverance. The only way to build up perseverance is to go through difficult situations, and so the cycle continues.

You see, James is saying that we should find joy in trials because we know the end of the story. Instead of focusing on the present darkness, we should look for the light at the end of the tunnel, and the longer we look at the light, the brighter the tunnel gets. When we try to consider eternity, it makes our struggles seem much smaller than when we are only focused on the present. Our times of trial are little more than blips on the timeline of God's Kingdom. Why waste our time being frustrated with our present state when we could be rejoicing over the work that is being done in our lives?

Ultimately, everything that happens is working toward the greater good of the Kingdom of God. That doesn't make it much easier in the moment, but if we can see through our pain to the light of the Kingdom that we are all working toward, then the joy of that hope will overwhelm any despair we may feel over the trials we face. It's not easy, but then nothing that is truly good is ever easy.

The Trinity

Now that we have a better idea of how to help new believers feel accepted, and a grasp of some of the behaviors that are important to faith, it's time we study one of the most foundational beliefs of Christianity. Studying the Bible in its context shows that Scripture is always pointing us to the big picture of the Kingdom of God. Even those verses that seem uniquely suited to our present situation also hold eternal value to an unlimited number of people. The Bible is a masterpiece that is persistently directing us to understand our roles and how we take part in the reality of the Kingdom.

Since that is the case, it is crucial that we seek the One that the Story is about. The doctrine of the Trinity is a foundational doctrine of Christianity, but that doesn't mean it is easy to understand. While we will never come to a complete grasp of the nuances of the belief that God is three-in-one, we still need to do our best to get a grip on this truth that provides the basis for our faith. It is through seeking to understand that we can continue to grow our relationship with God, and in doing so we can become appropriate participants in the Community and in Creation.

The doctrine of the Trinity is the belief that perhaps best embodies Job's declaration that "God is greater than we can understand" (Job 36:26). The doctrine is vital to the Christian faith because it explains the nature of God. It shows us how we can be brought back into communion with God and with others and, therefore, it gives us a foundational meaning for life.

From the beginning of our existence, humans have sought to understand and imitate the thoughts and actions of God, our Creator. We allowed ourselves to be convinced that to become like God we had to do that which He forbid us from doing, so we ate the fruit from the tree in the middle of the garden, and consequently, our attempt to become like God brought a curse and separation from Him we had not experienced before (Genesis 3).

Ever since that act of disobedience, our efforts to understand the nature of God have not ceased. These acts, which stemmed from a desire to restore intimacy with the Almighty, often came up short and we did not know how to deal with our sudden imperfection. It's important that we consider the path of understanding that Christians have taken as we have attempted to interpret the un-interpretable. This study of historical knowledge is another example of studying the context of our own beliefs to understand where we came from and avoid making some of the same mistakes.

THE DEVELOPMENT OF BELIEF

Gnosticism

Gnosticism was an early school of thought that sought to take hold of God with merely human knowledge, which meant that redemption for the Gnostics was found in knowledge of God rather than in forgiveness through Christ. First and second century Christians were faced with the task of explaining Christ's Divinity without sacrificing their belief in One God. In their attempt at doing so, Gnostics focused on what they could control. In other words, they attempted to understand God by expanding their minds as much as possible, as well as denying their bodies and earthly existence.

Gnosticism was an unending quest fueled by thinking more loftily than one ought to think. The Gnostics believed that redemption could be found through knowledge of the unspeakable majesty of God. The Gnostics had no problem blending polytheism and Christianity, complete with various systems of mythology and cosmology. The trademark of Gnosticism was a belief in secret knowledge. In an attempt to summarize what is a complex system of belief; the Gnostics believed that the secret knowledge, brought to earth by Jesus, included the revelation that the world was created by angelic beings known as *aeons*, and that the God of the Old Testament was simply one of these *aeons*. They also believed that the world was inherently evil, which led them to eventually deny Christ's humanity because they thought that even mere physical existence would have made Jesus' physical body evil.[31]

The Gnostics missed the point often. Among other things, their understanding of God was not the God that Christ preached; they did not understand evil to be a consequence of human sin but thought it was part of creation. Instead, they thought the salvation they should be seeking was not from sin but from the material world; and they largely disregarded Jesus' redemptive act in the Resurrection. [32]

Irenaeus, a first-century bishop who had a direct influence in many Church doctrines that are still adhered to, argued against the Gnostics by saying that God can only truly be known through Jesus Christ. He directly disagreed with the thought that angels had created the world, and affirmed the belief in one supreme God, with Creation being the image of God: "Creation shows its Creator, and what is made suggests its Maker."[33] He declared them blind and unable to find anything and completely contradicted their theology. Rather than focusing on human knowledge, Irenaeus presented an argument that sought to direct Christians toward Christ and influenced early theologians to seek God through what He has revealed to us in His Son. He exalted the role of the Son, and declared, "Everything became new when the Word, in a new

---

31 Papandrea, James Leonard. "The Church in the Subapostolic Age." *Reading the Early Church Fathers*, Paulist Press, 2012, pp. 66–75.

32 Papandrea, James Leonard. "The Church in the Subapostolic Age." *Reading the Early Church Fathers*, Paulist Press, 2012, pp. 73.

33 Irenaeus, *The Scandal of the Incarnation* (San Francisco: Ignatius Press. 1990), 33.

dispensation, came in the flesh to win back to God man who had gone off from God. Thus, men were taught to worship, not a different God, but the same God in a new way."[34]

Adoptionism

Adoptionism appeared in the second century as an attempt to explain how Christ could have been present among Creation without losing His Divinity. The adoptionist explanation took two forms: angel adoptionism and spirit adoptionism. Both arguments centered on the idea that Christ could not have been both divine and human.

Angel adoptionism claimed that Jesus of Nazareth, by perfect obedience, was justified by God and rewarded by being adopted as a son of God and given the gift of an indwelling angelic spirit. This spirit who lived in the human Jesus is called Christ, but even the spirit is not divine. Some adoptionists believed that the spirit, Christ, came into the human Jesus at the baptism, others believed it was at the time of conception, but both camps agreed that Jesus was merely an empowered human, but not divine in any way. This belief creates two separate entities: the indwelling angel (Christ) and the man (Jesus), both of whom were created and not divine[35].

Spirit adoptionism refers to the idea that it was the Holy Spirit that empowered the man Jesus of Nazareth. While the

34 Irenaeus, *The Scandal of the Incarnation* (San Francisco: Ignatius Press. 1990), 30-46.

35 James L. Papandrea, *The Earliest Christologies* (Downers Grove, Illinois: InterVarsity Press. 2016), 23-32.

mainstream church affirms that the Spirit was a gift from Jesus Christ, spirit adoptionists believed that Jesus was merely a recipient of the Holy Spirit. Like angel adoptionism, spirit adoptionism states that Jesus was rewarded for moral righteousness by being adopted by God at the baptism, when the Christ Spirit descended on Jesus and entered into him. Like the angel adoptionists, Jesus was believed to be a mere human, not at all unique among humanity apart from the gift of the indwelt Spirit. They rejected Jesus' divinity because they believed that he could not have been born, grew, learned, and died while being divine.[36]

The First Council of Nicaea rejected this claim in 325 (the Council of Nicaea was a meeting of many bishops who were brought together to come up with an official doctrine of the Trinity). The Council rejected both forms of adoptionism because they denied the divinity of Jesus, and Jesus had to be divine for Him to offer forgiveness. Essentially, the bishops said that the Son had to be fully human because becoming an actual, physical part of Creation is the only way God could have died and made atonement for our sins. It is necessary for God to be willing to fully participate in Creation in order to offer forgiveness.[37]

36 James L. Papandrea, *The Earliest Christologies* (Downers Grove, Illinois: InterVarsity Press. 2016), 33-43.

37 James L. Papandrea, *The Earliest Christologies* (Downers Grove, Illinois: InterVarsity Press. 2016), 23-32.

The Spirit-Fighters

In the third and fourth centuries, there was a group whose pneumatology (beliefs regarding the Holy Spirit) denied the divinity of the Spirit because they thought such a claim was a form of polytheism. These 'pneumatomachians' or 'Spirit-fighters', also known as Macedonians, claimed that if all three persons are divine, then Christianity is nothing but a form of tri-theism.

The chief objection to this view came from Gregory of Nyssa, a fourth-century bishop whose teachings informed much of our current doctrine of the Trinity. He responded to the Spirit-fighters by affirming that the Holy Spirit enjoyed the same consubstantiality (this is just a big, fancy word that means that each Person of the Trinity was of the same substance; basically, all Three are Divine) with the Father as does the Son. Essentially, Gregory argued that calling the Holy Spirit Divine was not a form of tri-theism because the Spirit is of the same divine nature as the Father and the Son and therefore worthy of worship. [38]

CONNECTION

Why does all this matter?

It matters because these beliefs, and many more like them, are the context from which we have come to our current understanding of the Trinity. Because of misplaced beliefs like we have just discussed, we now have a Trinitarian doctrine that is

---

38 James L. Papandrea, *Reading the Early Church Fathers* (New York: Paulist Press. 2012), 210-211.

more certain of what is *not* than what *is*, which isn't necessarily a bad thing. These ideas were important because they led to conversations and councils that allowed Christians not only to create doctrines, but also to reject those characteristics that cannot be true about our God. These attempts to explain God are what allowed us to determine the beliefs that are essential to our faith. Councils like Nicaea have allowed us the opportunity today to wrestle with who God is and how God works in the world and in our lives because they focused on rejecting false doctrine rather than trying to define God in totality. By defining what God is *not*, our predecessors were effectually admitting that they did not entirely know what God *is*, and that makes it much easier to continue the discussion today.

So, just how does the Trinity work together? And what does that have to do with us?

It has taken thousands of years of councils, individuals, and philosophy to develop what we currently accept as the doctrine of the Trinity, and it would be impossible to summarize such a belief in a concise manner. This book is not the place to grapple with the difficulties that come with any intense discussion of the Trinity. Instead, let's focus on how we can see the Trinity working to introduce the Kingdom to Creation. How can such a complex belief be immediately relevant to us, and how does this belief invite us to be children of God?

In this chapter, we will look at the doctrinal beliefs regarding the Father, the Son, and the Holy Spirit. We will discuss how the Trinity presents the Kingdom of God, and how the activity between the Trinity invites us to play a part in that Kingdom. We will also talk about how we can build a scriptural account of the Trinity, even though the Bible never directly references God as Trinity.

Christians state that "we believe in one God, the Father, the Almighty" and yet, despite our declaration of there being only one God, we also claim a belief in "one Lord, Jesus Christ, the only son of God" and another Lord, "the Holy Spirit, the Lord, the giver of life." [39] Though we seem to be contradicting ourselves by presenting a polytheistic view consisting of three gods, what we are actually affirming is a Triune Godhead made up of three persons but one substance; *tres persona, una substantia*. What we call the 'persons' of the Trinity indicate the distinction between the Father, Son, and Spirit while maintaining the unity of one God. Therefore, we believe that God exists as one divine substance in three divine persons. [40]"There is one Person of the Father; another of the Son; and another of the Holy Ghost. But the Godhead of the Father, of the Son, and of the Holy Ghost, is all one."[41]

THREE PERSONS, ONE SUBSTANCE

There are a multitude of resources that will dive deeper into the inner workings of the Trinity than I wish to with this book. Here, I am merely trying to present my understanding of how each person of the Trinity is presenting the Kingdom of God, and how they work together to do so. One resource

---

39 Nicene Creed

40 James L. Papandrea, *Reading the Early Church Fathers* (New York: Paulist Press. 2012), 102-103.

41 Athanasian Creed

for further study, that has informed much of this chapter, is *Delighting in the Trinity*, a book by Michael Reeves that truly is an introduction to the Christian faith. I suggest that if you wish a more complete analysis of this complex belief, you turn to Reeves' in its entirety.

For now, let's work through the Father, the Son, and the Spirit and how each individually works in us and turns us toward the Divine, and then turn to how we may actively participate in the Community which the Trinity is presenting.

As we move through this section, let's keep in mind that in any conversation about the Trinity, or any other aspect of Christianity, we are doing what David said in Psalm 27. We are gazing upon the beauty of the Lord and seeking His face.

THE FATHER

Church doctrine describes God the Father as the "Almighty, maker of heaven and earth, of all that is, seen and unseen." He made us, and not only us but all things. And yet He is not just Creator, but He is also Father. In the Bible we see that God as Father means that He is the "Father to the fatherless" (Ps. 68:5), "God our Father, who created all the lights in heaven" (James 1:17), and "our merciful Father and the source of all comfort" (2 Cor. 1:3). He is "over all, in all, and living through all" (Eph. 4:6) and, most importantly, He is one. Matthew goes as far as to tell us, "don't address anyone here on earth as 'Father,' for only God in heaven is your Father" (Matt. 23:9). That seems like a pretty outlandish suggestion, and I'm sure millions of dads around the world would be likely to balk at such a claim, so what could Matthew have meant?

It's safe to say that Matthew was not throwing dirt on our earthly fathers, but instead was exalting the Heavenly Father to a place of authority over that of any man. But if it's nothing more than a place of authority, why would that be a good thing? Because the Father's authority over earthly fathers is not based merely on power, but also on love. The first and greatest commandment is to love the Lord our God, but we can't love God if He is nothing more than Ruler. We can even ask the question: why would we want to?

The Father sent the Son to lead us to Him. Jesus Christ is the Way to the Father. Since Jesus is the Son, that means that God is primarily Father. This is jumping ahead a little, but the relationship within the Trinity is what we're here to discuss anyway, so why not jump ahead? If we understand God to be primarily Father, then we need to read the Bible as a presentation of all the things that the Father has done. From Old to New Testament, God is Father, and all His ways are beautiful in that light. So, if He is Father, what does that mean to us?

God is Father, which means that He has children. Good news here: we are His children! Some of us might shrink from such a claim, but to those I encourage you that God is more than a greater version of your dad. He is, in addition to being Father, love. He is love, and therefore all His actions are made from Fatherly love. As the French Reformer John Calvin wrote,

"To conclude once and for all, whenever we call God the creator of heaven and earth, let us at the same time bear in mind that… we are indeed his children, whom he has received into his faithful protection to nourish and educate." [42]

What Calvin describes is beautiful. Here is a Father offering us protection from all harm and in that protection, He wants to nourish and educate us. This is a Father free from all failures of morality or otherwise, desiring to envelope His children with His love. He so desires to love and protect His children that He has been doing it since the beginning. Look at what Jesus tells us in John 17:24: "Father, I want these whom you have given me to be with me where I am. Then they can see all the glory you gave me because you loved me even before the world began." You see, God as primarily Father means that before He even created the world, the Father loved the Son. Before He is ever Creator, He is a Father that loves His children.

"That proves that the Father loves the Son, and I guess I see how the Father creating us means He loves us, but are we really His children?"

Yes! In fact, it is in the very loving of the Son that the Father reveals His love for all Creation. So without further ado, let's turn now to our discussion of the Son.

---

42 John Calvin, *Institutes of the Christian Religion* 1.14.2

THE SON

Doctrinally, the Son is "the only-begotten son of the Father. He is the Lord, Jesus Christ, and is of one being with the Father. It is through the Son that the Father made all things. The Son became a man and was born of the Virgin Mary. He was crucified for our sake; He suffered death and was buried before rising again on the third day. The Son is now seated at the right hand of the Father, from where He will come to judge the living and the dead." [43]

"But what does all that academic mumbo-jumbo have to do with anything?"

Actually, quite a bit. We just have to do a little digging.

God as Son, as we have already discussed, means that there is a Father. We've already seen that God as Father means He has children, and God is love so that means He loves His children. But how does God as Son relate to us? We're about to find out.

Let's look at some Biblical characteristics of the Son.

Often when the Bible describes the Son, it is from the viewpoint of the Father. The Father calls the Son, "dearly loved" (Matt. 3:17, 17:5, Mark 1:11), and His "Chosen One" (Luke 9:35). The Son is affirmed as "full of unfailing love and faithfulness" (John 1:14), "a sacrifice to take away our sins" (1 John 4:10), our "advocate who pleads our case before the Father" (1 John 2:1), the "champion who initiates and perfects our faith" (Hebrews 12:2) the self-described "bread of life" (John 6:35), and these descriptions are just scratching

---

43 Nicene Creed

the surface of all the Bible tells us about the Son. These characteristics can help us know who we are talking about, but we have to consider some different things to figure out how the Son is working to invite us to take part in His Kingdom.

To see how the Son is working to extend a hand of grace to us, it helps to consider how exactly the Father felt about His Son. Simply put, the Father loves the Son deeply and eternally. Not only does the Father call the Son beloved, that love is affirmed to be eternal by the Son when He says, "Father…you loved me even before the world began" (John 17:24).

What we can see from this love is that Jesus Christ is the retelling of the story of Creation. Jesus is not just the Son, He is the "firstborn among many brothers" (Rom. 8:29). You see, the Father's love for the Son is so great that it cannot be contained and naturally overflows to all of creation. We can see this in the description of Christ as the inheritor of all things (Heb. 1:2) and our relation to that inheritance as "heirs of God's glory" together with Christ (Rom. 8:17). The opportunities that the Father has presented to the Son are also presented to us, because of the Son.

That is all well and good, in fact it is joyous in its allowance for grace, but it also presents a problem. It's easy to see how Christ deserves to be called an heir of God, but what about us? None of us have lived purely righteous lives, so why should we deserve to be co-heirs with the blameless Son of God?

Well, we don't deserve it. Our rejection of God's original offer of a relationship with Him, which we made clear in our disobedience, made it necessary for an act of grace to restore our communion with the Father. Thus, we find the most astonishing aspect of the Story of God in that despite our rejection, our disobedience, our insubordination against our Father, He still creates an opportunity for redemption.

"God showed how much he loved us by sending his one and only Son into the world so that we might have eternal life through him. This is real love—not that we loved God, but that he loved us and sent his Son as a sacrifice to take away our sins."
1 John 4:9-10

WHY WOULD GOD DO SUCH A THING?

As Jesus reveals, the Father sent the Son to make Himself known and to share the love that is between them with us (John 17). The Son's very existence is to reveal the Father to His Creation. We are the recipients of undeserved grace and love. And with that grace and love comes the chance to experience the inheritance that is due Christ, the inheritance of the Kingdom and of communion with the Father.

No matter how much time we devote to making sense of this love, it's a difficult pill to swallow. It is not difficult because of anything the Father has done, but because of our own guilt. It is just hard to imagine a Father so loving that, despite generations of rejection, He still offers forgiveness and a chance to experience all that is His. This is something we can only hope to understand by the nudging of that third Person, the Holy Spirit. But, before we get to the Spirit, it's important that we look at how the Father and Son are working to present the Spirit, and how the Spirit works to do the same.

C.S. Lewis writes on the Trinity and offers a provocative

explanation by saying: "The union between the Father and Son is such a live and concrete thing that this union itself is also a Person."[44] He goes on to explain that what he means is similar to the 'spirit' that people speak of when they talk about a group, family, team, or club. He says that people talk about its "spirit" because "the individual members, when they are together, do really develop particular ways of talking and behaving which they would not have if they were apart."[45]

Now, in the instances that Lewis is describing that "spirit" would of course not relate to a real person. But Lewis says that is just another of the differences between God and us, because in the life of the Father and the Son there is a real Person, and that third Person is the Holy Spirit. That's a little bit difficult to wrap a human mind around, but what we need to see is that the love of the Father and Son is so intense that it needs a third Person to describe it, and that Person is just as real as the Father and Son. What we need to see from Lewis' explanation is that the Spirit is borne out of the love of the Father and Son, that the Spirit is just as real and just as Personal as the Father and Son, and we need to recognize that the Spirit is eternal and has existed just as long as the Father and Son have existed, since their love has always existed.

Let's move now to consider what the Bible reveals to us about the Spirit, and how the Spirit works to invite us into the Kingdom.

---

44 Lewis, Clive Staples. "The Trinity." *The Joyful Christian*, Macmillan Publishing, 1977, pp. 45–48.

45 Lewis, Clive Staples. "The Trinity." *The Joyful Christian*, Macmillan Publishing, 1977, pp. 45–48.

THE HOLY SPIRIT

The Bible teaches us much about the Spirit. We know that he will teach us and remind of us of the things that Jesus taught us (John 14:26), He helps us in our weakness, and intercedes for us when we do not know what to pray (Rom. 8:26), and He bears witness that we are children of God (Rom. 8:16). We also know that the Spirit is a gift from the Son: "If you love me, obey my commandments. And I will ask the Father, and he will give you another Advocate, who will never leave you. He is the Holy Spirit" (John 14:15-17). The Spirit is given to us by the Father, through the Son, so let's consider what that means regarding our relationship to the Spirit.

To do so, let's glance at Reeves' *Delighting in the Trinity*:

> *"Through the giving of the Spirit, God shares with us – and catches us up into – the life that is his. The Father has eternally known and loved his great Son, and through the Spirit he opens our eyes so that we too might know him, and so he wins our hearts that we too might love him…In other words, through the Spirit the Father allows us to share in the enjoyment of what most delights him – his Son."* [46]

The Spirit's work in our lives is to bring us to Christ and share in the enjoyment of the Son. This work does more than just bring us to Christ, it allows us to be united to Christ. The Spirit takes what is Christ's and makes it ours (John 16:14). So it is only by the Spirit that we can hope to experience the

---

46 Reeves, Michael. "The Christian Life." *Delighting in the Trinity*, IVP Academic, 2012, pp. 94.

inheritance we talked about in the last section. Just as we have seen that it is by the Spirit that the Father has eternally loved the Son, it is also by the Spirit that the Father desires to invite us to experience that same love.

The Spirit's existence is a testament to God's desire to draw near to His creation. "He unites us to the Son so that together we cry 'Abba' and begin to know each other truly as brothers and sisters."[47] The Spirit turns us toward the Son, who in turn reveals the Father to us. That little tug on your heart telling you to listen to a specific part of a sermon, or to speak to someone on the street, or to do anything that you otherwise wouldn't have considered is often a revelation of the work of the Spirit that is drawing you to be more like Christ.

THREE-IN-ONE

The Holy Spirit is God's provision for us to be able to communicate and feel the presence of God in our earthly lives. The Three work together to provide a chance for us to have a life worth living. It is this hope that we strive for, and it is reaffirmed throughout history by the Trinity. The Spirit prepares us for the Son, the Son leads us to the Father, and the Father offers us eternal life. The Three work as one in the allowance and bestowing of forgiveness on Creation.[48]

C.S. Lewis describes the work of the Triune Godhead by

---

47 Reeves, Michael. "The Christian Life." *Delighting in the Trinity*, IVP Academic, 2012, pp. 103.

48 Irenaeus, *The Scandal of the Incarnation* (San Francisco: Ignatius Press. 1990), 47-52.

asking us to consider a Christian when he prays:

> *"An ordinary simple Christian kneels down to say his prayers. He is trying to get in touch with God. But if he is a Christian he knows that what is prompting him to pray is also God: God, so to speak, inside him. But he also knows that all his real knowledge of God comes through Christ, the Man who was God — that Christ is standing beside him, helping him to pray, praying for him. You see what is happening. God is the thing to which he is praying — the goal he is trying to reach. God is also the thing inside him which is pushing him on — the motive power. God is also the road or bridge along which he is being pushed to that goal. So that the whole threefold life of the three-personal Being is actually going on in that ordinary little bedroom where an ordinary man is saying his prayers."* [49]

In the activity between the Father, Son, and Spirit, it is obvious that God desires relationships between beings. The Father enjoys the relations between Himself so much that He wishes to share that fellowship with those who He would create. The Son is willing and eager to share the love of the Father with us. As Reeves concludes, the Spirit gives us Himself so that we can share the satisfaction of knowing Him. "Far, far from theological clutter, God's being Father, Son and Spirit is

---

49 Lewis, Clive Staples. "The Three-Personal God." *The Joyful Christian*, Macmillan Publishing, 1977, pp. 43–45

just what makes the Christian life beautiful." [50]

The Trinity is the ultimate thing to be enjoyed, so we should study with a sense of joy rather than frustration, and we should discuss with an intention to understand rather than to be proven right. It is in the Father that we find unity, in the Son that we find equality, and in the Holy Spirit that we find harmony. It is only through God that we may perceive the light of unchanging wisdom for Wisdom was willing to adapt Himself to our weakness and make Himself the way by which we may contribute to the Kingdom. [51]

THE TRINITY IN THE SACRAMENTS

We briefly discussed the sacraments earlier, but it's important to note how our attempts at understanding the Trinity, already written down in creeds and doctrines, are also acted out in the sacraments of Christianity. These actions are how we interact with the Trinity, and how we provide public testimonies to our faith.

Just as the Trinity is evident in the baptism of Christ, we continue to act out our victory over death in our own baptisms. We are accepting Christ's forgiveness by renouncing the corruption of death and accepting a new beginning in Christ. In baptism, we are joined to Christ's sufferings and are thereby able to experience the reality of salvation even though we do not really die, we are not really buried, and we are not

---

50 Reeves, Michael. "The Christian Life." *Delighting in the Trinity*, IVP Academic, 2012, pp. 85–107.

51 Augustine, *On Christian Doctrine*, §5-11.

really crucified and raised again. Yet, it is by our imitation of
Christ that we can share in His suffering for our sake and, in
that way, accept salvation.[52]

The Eucharist is perhaps the best picture of Community
in which we can actively participate. Christ proclaims the
Eucharist to be a creation of a new reality in which we can
participate. In taking Christ's body and blood, Christians are
united to Christ Himself. We are taking in a portion of Christ
and thus are receiving more of Him as well. In partaking of
His body and blood, we are becoming more like Him. It is
through faith that we affirm the elements of the Eucharist to
be the Body and Blood of Christ and how we determine that
through this action we are becoming "partakers of the Divine
nature." [53]

Furthermore, in taking communion together, we are also
engaging in a generational tradition that ties together Christians
from now all the way back to the Last Supper. It is an act of
coming together that should never be taken lightly and should
bring us insurmountable joy. In the Eucharist, we are reaching
out and accepting Christ's offer, not only of forgiveness, but also
participation in the Kingdom. We are accepting the invitation
to join a Community of believers that consists of way more
than we could ever picture or consider.

---

52 Cyril, *On Baptism*, §5-8.

53 Cyril, *On the Eucharist*, §1-6

CONCLUSION

With all this having been said and affirmed by generations of Christians, it is important that we realize that these beliefs are not necessarily concrete. Any attempt to understand God can only be taken with the humility of realizing that you will probably be wrong. Or, at the very least, not completely right. We are operating with only human knowledge, so there is simply no way that we can expect to be correct about all things regarding the Trinity. Anything that is meant for us to know completely will be revealed to us, all other knowledge should be explored without expectation of finding a final answer.

What we need to take from this discussion is the reality that God has constantly been working to maintain His Kingdom on earth, and we are offered the chance to be part of it. From Creation, through the Fall, through the Resurrection, and all the way to today, God has been piecing together this master-piece despite the difficulties we have made for ourselves. The work of the Trinity has magnificently provided a chance for Creation to experience the love of its Creator. Taking part in the eternal Community isn't easy, but it is simple. It starts with a realization of the offer before us that comes from experiencing God in every way that He has made available to us.

Verses In Context Part IV

JOHN 3:16

"For this is how God loved the world: He gave his one and only Son, so that everyone who believes in him will not perish but have eternal life."

Martin Luther, the German theologian credited with starting the Protestant Reformation, called John 3:16 the "Bible in miniature", and many Christians think it is the most important verse in the Bible. You see it on signs at football games and on bumper stickers while you're stuck in traffic. Let's dig deeper into what exactly is going on in John 3:16 and what makes it so influential.

CONTEXT

In John 3, Jesus is having a conversation with a man named Nicodemus. Nicodemus is an important figure in Jewish society; he's a Pharisee and a member of the Jewish ruling council – the Sanhedrin. As a Pharisee, he belongs to a group that were the spiritual fathers of Judaism and believed in a series of laws that were open to interpretation.[54] They were the religious conservatives and the main source of persecution against Jesus and His followers.

The Pharisees went as far as to tell everyone that Jesus got His power to perform miracles from "Satan, the prince of demons" (Matthew 12:24). But they didn't stop there. In fact, they were the men who convinced the Sadducees, another group of religious leaders who fear Jesus' influence, to have Jesus killed. Jesus responded to both groups with some of His most serious accusations, calling them "hypocrites" (Matt. 23:13) and even a "brood of snakes" (Matt. 12:34). Why were the two sides at odds with each other?

Jesus didn't agree with many of the rules that the Pharisees taught as law. He especially spoke against their desire to make themselves appear more religious than the rest of the community (Luke 11:37-54). The Pharisees were a 'holier-than-thou' group of hypocrites who were overly concerned with what everyone else thought, and Jesus wasn't quiet about his displeasure with their actions.

The Pharisees persecuted Jesus because He had been travelling the area performing miracles and teaching ideas that directly contradicted their own instruction. In fact, just a few days before Nicodemus went to see Him, Jesus had driven everyone out of the Temple with a homemade whip after seeing how they had turned a "house of prayer" into a "den of thieves" (Matt. 21:13). It doesn't make sense that Nicodemus

---

54 Mitchell G. Bard, *The Complete Idiot's Guide to Middle East Conflicts*, NY: MacMillan,1999.

would want to meet with the Sanhedrin's greatest adversary, yet that's exactly what Nicodemus decided to do.

Nicodemus came to Jesus at night, likely to minimize the chances of being seen meeting with Jesus. This is all taking place right around the time of Passover, the biggest Jewish holiday that celebrates the Jewish exodus from Egypt. And all this is taking place around Jerusalem, so there were millions of eyes that could have seen Nicodemus' risky meeting. When you consider all the risk involved, it's clear that Nicodemus did not take this meeting lightly. He had something of dire importance to discuss and he was willing to risk his reputation to get the answers he needed.

Upon Nicodemus' arrival, Jesus begins teaching him about the Kingdom of God. Jesus tells this Pharisee that he needs to be born of water (baptism) and of the Spirit to make it to the Kingdom. Nicodemus doesn't understand, so Jesus tells him that he will never understand heavenly things if he can't even comprehend the earthly things. Then Jesus launches into a paragraph of teaching about Himself, but He does so in such a way that Nicodemus wouldn't have immediately understood what was being said. Luckily, thousands of years later, we still have a chance to try to grasp the wisdom of the Son.

CONNECTION

This is where we find John 3:16, as Jesus tells Nicodemus that God sent His Son to save the world, not to judge the world, and that belief in the Son is what it takes to have eternal life. This claim would have been astonishing to a Pharisee who is used to telling people that they will be judged for what they do on earth, so we can imagine that Nicodemus went back to his home with a lot on his mind that night. But did Jesus' instruction change the way he acted?

Nicodemus is only mentioned twice more in the Bible but both times he takes Jesus' side against his former companions. In John 7, Nicodemus tries to defend Jesus while the other Pharisees are trying to determine whether and how to kill him. Then, after the Crucifixion, Nicodemus is one of the men who assists in preparing Jesus' body for burial by wrapping him in linens.

It's safe to say that this moonlit meeting in John 3 was enough to convince Nicodemus that Jesus is the Son of God.

So, what does that mean for us?

It means that we need to be as self-aware as Nicodemus, and realize that we don't know it all. Nicodemus was extremely intelligent and held a high position of authority in Jewish society, but even he realized that he didn't have it all figured out and that he needed answers only Jesus could provide. He came to Jesus with his questions, and Jesus answered those questions before he could even ask.

Nicodemus is like all of us, and Jesus' teaching can help us grasp how marvelous God's love is that He was willing to send His Son to die for a Creation that doesn't deserve that love. It is this love revealed in the Incarnation that the Bible is showing us from start to finish. Christ made the ultimate sacrifice of His life, and the Father made the ultimate sacrifice of giving His Son's life for the sake of ours. That's something that should never be taken for granted, and it is the main point of not only John 3:16, but the entire Bible.

There is something much more complex at stake in this verse than we could possibly imagine. Without the love described in John 3:16, we would only be waiting for eventual judgment. We would have no hope of salvation nor could we even begin to comprehend how true love might look. It is only through the love described in John 3:16 that we can have any chance of a relationship with God.

We might think we know it all, but we need to quit focusing on what we do know and try our best to continually learn more about the love God has for us, because that is something that we can spend our lives doing. If we are willing to put everything aside and head into the night to learn more from the mouth of Jesus Christ, then we just might stand a chance of playing a meaningful part in the Kingdom and spending eternity with God.

2 CORINTHIANS 12:9

"Each time he said, "My grace is all you need. My power works best in weakness." So now I am glad to boast about my weaknesses, so that the power of Christ can work through me."

It's likely that 2 Corinthians 12:9 has served as an important source of hope for many people searching for light during a dark time. These words from Jesus, shared by Paul, provide strength to those who are feeling disappointed. When someone feels like there's nothing left for them, Jesus says His grace is sufficient; and when they feel like they have no power left, Jesus says that His power will break through and be made perfect in weakness.

Maybe that's all most people need to hear, but the verse doesn't stop there. Paul goes on to offer some of his own insight and explain why he boasts in his weaknesses as opportunities for Christ's power to rest on him. While the first part of this verse is cited often, Paul's input is less popular. He might not have been the Son, but Paul was an exceptional catalyst in the development of Christianity, so it's imperative that we consider what he had to say.

CONTEXT

The book of 2 Corinthians is one of several letters that Paul wrote to the church in Corinth. The writings contained in 2 Corinthians were probably written around the year 55 A.D., or about 20 years after the death and resurrection of Christ.

Paul is writing to a church that he knew well, and is writing in the early stages of the growth of the faith. In this letter, it's clear that he is writing partly to explain himself and defend his authority to speak on issues within the church, as well as to teach and encourage his readers to live Christian lifestyles.

[55]Leading into chapter 12, Paul defends his ministry, and begins to teach the Corinthians how to deal with opposition in the church. He boasts about the sufferings he has gone through because of his willingness to follow Christ, and shares stories of others who have gone through similar difficulties. He ends his boasting by giving Christ all the credit and says that the only reason he does boast is so that Christ's power may rest on him.

CONNECTION

It might seem like Paul is just building himself up to look good in the eyes of his audience. After all, he does spend a lot of time talking about what all he has gone through to spread the Gospel around the world. But after all this storytelling, Paul recognizes that the source of his strength was always Christ.

"Then why does he spend so much time talking about himself?"

A theme in many of Paul's letters is his defense of his ministry. He's not bragging about anything, he is giving proof that he knows what he is talking about and that his teachings should be taken seriously because of his experiences. In fact, if you investigate any section of Scripture where Paul is bragging about his suffering, he always makes it clear that it isn't his own

---

55 "Intro to 2 Corinthians." *Biblica*, Zondervan, 9 Oct. 2016, www.biblica. com/resources/scholar-notes/niv-study-bible/intro-to-2-corinthians/.

power getting him through his sufferings, it is always Christ. In 2 Corinthians 12, he mentions a time when he says the Lord told him that his "grace is all you need."

Paul goes on to say that he will continue to boast in his human weaknesses because it is through those weaknesses that Christ makes his power evident. That doesn't mean life is going to be easy. In fact, to put ourselves in situations where our weaknesses are made evident, we are going to have to experience some uncomfortable times. It is in those "weaknesses, insults, hardships, persecutions, and troubles" that we should be able to boast even more strongly, for Christ's sake. As we boast more on Christ's power, we will find that difficult situation is easier to get through as we allow Christ to work in our weakness.

The Christian life is about much more than our present struggles, but everyday struggles allow us the chance to boast about Christ's power constantly. We can defeat whatever life may throw at us because we know that Christ is working in us to give us the strength we need to make it through each day. Just like Paul says, we should keep in mind whose strength we have in us and thereby delight in difficulties, because when we are weak, then we are strong.

EPHESIANS 2:8-9

"God saved you by his grace when you believed. And you can't take credit for this; it is a gift from God. Salvation is not a reward for the good things we have done, so none of us can boast about it."

If you've ever found yourself in a position where it feels like you can't do anything right, there's a decent chance someone has quoted Ephesians 2:8-9 to let you know that it's okay, because you are saved by grace despite your unworthiness. It's simple to take such a verse and turn it into an excuse to sit around and not do anything – after all, we aren't saved by our works – but that's clearly missing the point.

It isn't entirely incorrect to take this verse from Paul's letter to the church in Ephesus as an assurance to not worry about our shortcomings. But is it taking the liberty of grace too far to understand the verse to mean we should never worry about what we do under any circumstances?

CONTEXT

The book of Ephesians is another of Paul's letters to a group of believers to educate them on the basics of the faith. This letter, while addressed to the church in Ephesus, was probably written to be spread among many churches in the area. So while we could say that these teachings were meant for one specific group of believers, it's more likely that Paul was purposefully writing in a way that would relate to the larger community.

It is important to note that Paul is writing while he is imprisoned, either in Caesarea or in Rome, and he is writing to a city in Ephesus that is a leading center in the Roman Empire.

"Wait a second, why was Paul in prison?"

Paul was in prison often and, while it's difficult to know precisely how long, how often, and the actual reason stated by his captors, it's safe to say that his immense influence on the region's religious landscape made him an enemy to all other religious and state leaders. Some Christians loved Paul, but most of them didn't due to his history of persecution against the believers with whom he came to align himself. He had a target on his back and, if we study his life, he was often held in prison as an attempt to just keep him quiet. That didn't work, clearly, and his letters still reached churches all around the ancient world.

In Ephesians, it's important to note that Paul knew many of his readers. He had visited Ephesus twice, and was a recognizable face to many of the other churches in the area, so this letter is based on a familiarity between Paul and his readers. [56]

CONNECTION

Paving the way to verses 8 and 9, Paul teaches his readers about their new life found in Christ. He says they were "dead because of [their] sins" but given life in Christ's resurrection. Paul is introducing a key concept of the Christian faith by teaching

---

56 Malick, David. "An Introduction To The Book Of Ephesians." *Bible. org*, 8 July 2004, bible.org/article/introduction-book-ephesians.

his readers how Christ continues to affect their lives. He ends this portion of his letter by ensuring that his readers know just who is responsible for their salvation – "it is the gift of God."

Paul isn't telling his readers that they have nothing to worry about, and if you continue to read Ephesians you'll see that he goes on to outline numerous lifestyle guidelines that should be followed by "Children of the Light." The apostle is introducing the Christian faith and establishing the foundation on which the rest of the letter, and all of Christianity, finds its stability.

Ephesians 2:8-9 is an important verse because it provides a basic tenet of Christianity, and it is a truth that cannot be overlooked. If we don't understand that our salvation is found in grace, and not anything we did to deserve it, then we overlook the gift that Christ gave us with his life. We have not done anything to deserve salvation, so we should understand that it is something given to us even though we are unworthy.

"Wow, that's a big deal. What do we do with that?"

When we can come to accept our salvation as a gift of grace, we can lose our desire to boast about how great we are. Our boasting turns from ourselves to Christ, and that is something that makes this verse even more important. You see, when our speech turns from ourselves to Christ, we are doing our part for the eternal Kingdom that belongs to Christ.

Maybe you would rather boast about how great you are and not spend your life only talking about what Jesus has done for you. I get that. I like talking about things that I've done well too, because it makes me feel good. The thing is, when our time on earth ends, is it more important for the name of Jesus to be remembered or our own name?

That's a question we all must face, so it's a good thing that Ephesians 2:8-9 gives us an answer.

The Finale

The verses we have engaged with were not meant to be an exhaustive dissection but an introduction to the study of Scripture in context. Hopefully, they have presented a path of interpretation that takes into consideration the contextual, historical, genre-specific aspects of Scripture, and apply those in relation to the lasting meaning of the Bible. Doing so shows the overwhelming theme of community that is portrayed throughout the Bible and is also an act as part of that community.

The story of Creation shows God's desire for humans to have companionship. Noah and the Ark is proof that life in the Kingdom is about what is best for the whole of humanity rather than the individual. The story of the Exodus is a representation of God's willingness to redeem us to Himself according to our obedience and desire to worship Him. The history of Israel is littered with God proving Himself to be a good and loving Creator that is eager to bring us into communion with Him and with each other. The story of Jonah is another example that God is more concerned with the spreading of the Word for the good of all humanity than with our individual desires.

And these are just a few examples. The Bible is riddled with stories of individuals who were used by God for the good of the Community, and they are lessons of how God can use us if we are obedient. Whether our obedience comes quickly and often or only once in our lives, God knows exactly what we are capable of and how we can make a difference as part of the collective. Scripture as an invitation to the Community is a conversation that could go on forever because of the vast number of stories in the Bible that serve as further proof that Scripture is meant to bring each member of the Kingdom together.

The Bible is more than just a personal instruction manual meant to help the individual navigate existence without any major mishaps. Rather, Scripture is more of a guidebook that tells us that we are not going to get through life alone, and we don't have to. Even in those moments when we feel we have no one on Earth who could possibly empathize with our situation, Scripture provides us generations of individuals who know exactly what we are going through, if not on a physical level at least on a spiritual level. The Community that God is inviting us to take part in is everlasting and extends from the first man through every person who has ever been born. We are all playing a part in the Kingdom.

For Christians, our desire needs to be one of community empowerment that is achieved in part by deepening our own understanding and relationship with God. Our goal can never be one of self-advancement, but of communal advancement. If we learn nothing else from Scripture let us grasp this one thing; that life is not about the individual, it is about the collective.

All of humanity has an innate desire to be part of something bigger than themselves. Not everyone realizes that desire, but upon taking part in something that has significance beyond the present moment we may feel a sense of joy that was not there before. When we do something for someone else, we are fulfilling what Scripture is calling us to do; we are acting as part of the Community. We are fulfilling the desire that God has created us with to make something of lasting value, and that lasting value can come to fruition in our relationships with one another. Scripture provides us with the most lasting solution to our wish to extend our life beyond our time on earth, and that is to play a role in the only eternal kingdom, the Kingdom of God.

From the very beginning, God has been acting in our lives and trying to show each individual that this life is not about you, it's about us.

WELCOME TO THE KINGDOM

Throughout this book, we have seen the importance of contextual biblical interpretation, and we have explored the possibilities that come from such study. No matter how much we want to make it about our own lives, the Bible is the Story of the Kingdom of God. When we realize this, we are able to react accordingly. That means extending grace to all those who are seeking the face of the same God we are after. It means understanding ourselves and why what we do as a Church is important. It also means engaging with our beliefs in an intimate and honest way. Belief in God is not easy, but it can be simple if we focus on the things that truly matter. We have an invitation before us to be part of the only eternal Community, and that's an amazing opportunity that we can't just pass up.

I hope this book has been intriguing enough to compel you to further study. The Bible is complex and contradictory, and yet it can be so simple and straightforward. The words which we find in the Holy Scripture are truly lamps lighting our path to the Father. They are the guideposts by which we may experience God in Trinity. I hope that you have seen the value that can come with determining the original impact of each verse and how that extra step is really a way of simplifying the text to what it originally meant, and I hope that by doing so you have seen the marvelous works of God that reveal His desire for us to spend eternity with Him. The Bible is not about us, but it is a grand invitation for us to join the most overwhelming, breathtaking Kingdom that has ever or will ever exist.

There is more to life than what is right in front of us. There is an incomprehensible depth to God, so it is impossible to assume that we can ever fully understand His word or His world. If the Good News is Christ's Resurrection, then the Great News might be that we don't have to understand Christ to love Christ. To love Christ is to love our neighbor and to love our neighbor is to accept one another despite any differences there may be between us. This is the call of Christ on our lives – to deny ourselves, follow Him, love one another unconditionally, and to recognize that this life is not about you or me or him or her or any one person, but that it is about all of us seeking to find the One who has made us all. In Scripture, God invites us to take part in His Kingdom by forgetting our own ambitions. In this way, we can achieve more than we ever imagined. This invitation from God is infinite in both distance and time, and it says to all of us:

Welcome to the Kingdom.

Acknowledgements

Mom & Pops, your support and encouragement has always been invaluable. Thank you for pushing me to be my best and to chase my dreams.

Hank, thank you for helping me out while writing a dissertation and thank you for being a big part of my growth during my college years.

Clayton and **Clayton**, thank you for your work in helping this dream become a reality.

Made in the USA
Columbia, SC
18 January 2019